A GUIDE TO BUILDING SUSTAINABLE ORGANIZATIONS FROM THE INSIDE OUT

AN ORGANIZATIONAL CAPACITY-BUILDING TOOLBOX FROM THE CHICAGO FOUNDATION FOR WOMEN

An Organization-Building Workbook
from
The Chicago Foundation for Women
230 West Superior
Chicago, IL 60610-3536
www.cfw.org

and

The Asset-Based Community Development Institute
Institute for Policy Research
Northwestern University
2040 Sheridan Road
Evanston, IL 60208-4100
www.northwestern.edu/IPR/abcd.html

Deborah L. Puntenney, Ph.D.

Chicago Foundation for Women Staff Contributors:
Christine H. Grumm, Executive Director
Linda Harlan, Program Director
Maria Mangual, Director of Development
Tina Battle, Communications Director

Distributed exclusively by:
ACTA Publications
4848 North Clark Street
Chicago, IL 60640
Phone: 800-397-2282
Fax: 800-397-0079
Email: acta@one.org

NOTE FROM THE CHICAGO FOUNDATION FOR WOMEN

The Chicago Foundation for Women would like to take this opportunity to thank readers and users of this guide for their interest and support of the work. Based on its experiences with the Sustainability of Healthy Organizations for Women in the 21st Century (SHOW-21) program, the foundation believes the model and tools presented here will prove useful for a variety of organizations implementing the process. As part of their ongoing commitment to supporting organizations that address the concerns of women and girls, the foundation will use the proceeds from this workbook to establish a fund from which to provide support to grantees using the assets approach in their organization-building efforts. As a purchaser of this volume, you have helped to make this fund a reality. Thank you for your support.

ACKNOWLEDGEMENTS

The Chicago Foundation for Women would like to acknowledge the involvement and extensive contributions to this workbook made by the participants in the original working group of the Sustainability of Healthy Organizations for Women in the 21st Century (SHOW-21) program. The organizations listed were selected to be part of SHOW-21 because of their excellent reputations in the Chicago nonprofit community and because they were viewed as having worthwhile experiences and knowledge to contribute to the work on organizational sustainability. The primary participant is listed in each case, as well as alternates who were deeply involved during the first 18 months of the program.

Chicago Abortion Fund—Toni Bond, Executive Director

Housing Opportunities for Women—Britt Shawver, Executive Director; Jeanne Zimmer, Associate Executive Director

Illinois Caucus for Adolescent Health—Jenny Knauss, Executive Director; Wendy Fegenhols, Board President

Mujeres Latinas en Acción—Norma Seledón, Executive Director; Doris Salomón, Board President

Older Women's League of Illinois—Lisa January, Executive Director

Rape Victim Advocates—Jerri Lynn Fields, Executive Director

Sisterhouse—La Donna Redmond, Executive Director

The Center for Impact Research (formerly the Taylor Institute)—Rebekah Levin, Deputy Director

The Enterprising Kitchen—Joan Pikas, Executive Director; Ann Jenich, Associate Director

Women in the Director's Chair—Rebecca Gee, Executive Director

In addition, the Chicago Foundation for Women would like to acknowledge the contributions made by members of the Asset-Based Community Development Institute (ABCD) of Northwestern University to the original thinking upon which the SHOW-21 program was based. John McKnight and John Kretzmann of the ABCD Institute have developed a new way of thinking about community development that emphasizes the assets and capacities of local people as the key to successful engagement of citizens. The SHOW-21 program was designed to utilize and expand on this focus in the context of building organizational sustainability. Deborah Puntenney, Director of Research and Publications at ABCD, was invited by the foundation to work with the SHOW-21 program because of her eight years of experience with the institute.

The foundation acknowledges the ongoing work of members of its staff and board on the SHOW-21 program. In particular, Carolyn Garrett, Cat Jefcoat, and Joyce Love made important contributions.

Finally, the foundation would like to acknowledge the funders who have provided support for the SHOW-21 program. These include **The Chicago Community Trust**, **The Frances P. Rohlen Fund of the Chicago Foundation for Women**, **Polk Bros. Foundation**, and **The Siegel Foundation**.

The art on the cover of this publication was designed by Valerie Lorimer.

ABOUT THE CHICAGO FOUNDATION FOR WOMEN

The Chicago Foundation for Women (CFW) is a nonprofit, public grantmaking foundation dedicated to increasing resources, expanding opportunities, and promoting positive social change for women and girls. The foundation raises funds, provides grants for programs serving women and girls, and advocates increased giving among other resources.

The Chicago Foundation for Women is a partnership of donors, grantees, volunteers, and staff working together, acting as catalysts, and fostering connections to promote positive social change for women and girls, their families and communities. These women and men come together—bringing their assets and vision—to support the foundation in its grantmaking and advocacy efforts. Thanks to this partnership, the Chicago Foundation for Women continues to impact the lives of millions of women and girls throughout metropolitan Chicago and the state of Illinois.

CFW supports programs that are solution-oriented, address root causes, are community-based, and create leadership opportunities for women and girls. Since 1986, the foundation has awarded close to 1,500 grants totaling more than $6 million to programs serving women and girls in the following issue areas: social and systems change advocacy; capacity building and organizational development; arts and culture; sexual assault and domestic violence; employment and economic development; girls; housing and homelessness; leadership development; physical and mental health; reproductive rights; and women's philanthropy. In addition to its focus on particular issue areas, CFW supports programs addressing the needs of immigrant and refugee women, incarcerated women, lesbians, older women, and women with disabilities.

SHOW-21 (Sustainability of Healthy Organizations for Women in the 21st Century) was formed out of CFW's commitment to being more than a grantmaker. The foundation understands that grants alone do not ensure the long-term viability of an organization. Therefore, its programs include grantee support through technical assistance, training, and leadership development.

CFW's staff, board, and community leaders provide technical assistance in partnership with our grantees as they build upon their own assets to strengthen their organizational capacities.

Through projects such as SHOW-21, CFW encourages women's groups to work collaboratively to expand opportunities and resources for women and girls. Together, we are strengthening communities by creating sustainable organizations that promote positive social change.

TABLE OF CONTENTS

INTRODUCTION

INTRODUCTION

Since 1986, the Chicago Foundation for Women (CFW) has invested in programs to improve the lives of women and girls thereby creating a better Chicago. The foundation's mission goes beyond grantmaking and incorporates work to educate the larger community about women and girls and their capacities and needs, develop women and girls as community leaders, support the development of women's organizations, and encourage these groups to work collaboratively. Part of CFW's mission is to invest in programs that improve the lives of women and girls by developing and releasing their capacity for full and equal participation in community life. As part of this ongoing commitment, CFW developed the Sustainability of Healthy Organizations for Women in the 21st Century (SHOW-21) program. Initiated in April 1998, SHOW-21 is examining ways to strengthen Chicago's community of women's organizations, exploring the reasons why some organizations have failed, and developing models to help women's organizations increase their sustainability. The SHOW-21 program is based on the assumption that sustainability can be achieved when organizations recognize and understand the full measure of their assets and capacities and then build upon them, generating strong relationships among the internal and external components of the organization's milieu.

Beginning in April 1998, CFW convened a working group of talented executive directors from among their grantee organizations to participate in a series of workshops designed to examine organizational sustainability within this framework and develop a new model for organizational practice. As a result of their organizational asset-mapping activities and collaborative exploration of asset-mobilizing opportunities, SHOW-21 participants simultaneously contributed to the development of this new model and tested it over a period of 18 months. As part of the model, the working group developed definitions and tools, identified key issues related to sustainability, and planned organizational capacity-building projects based on their asset-mapping activities. Unlike other models for strengthening organizations, which often focus on the search for funding, the SHOW-21 model broadens the focus to include systematic exploration and utilization of every aspect of an organization's many potential assets.

The SHOW-21 work has been part of an ongoing participatory action research and evaluation study that has tracked their efforts, progress, and outcomes. The results of this effort are especially exciting in that the participants made great strides in mobilizing their organizational assets toward increased sustainability *and* helped to produce a flexible but systematic way for other organizations to implement what they learned. This workbook illustrates the SHOW-21 model for increasing organizational sustainability and offers a series of activities and tools to other groups interested in this approach. It is presented with pride by the Chicago Foundation for Women in collaboration with the Asset-Based Community

Development Institute, the members of the SHOW-21 working group, the author, and the program's funders.

<u>A New Strategy for Nonprofit Development</u>

The SHOW-21 program was designed to expand on the work of the Asset-Based Community Development Institute of Northwestern University's Institute for Policy Research and apply its principles and practices to organizational settings. Kretzmann and McKnight's work on asset-based community development has heretofore been used as a set of strategies for building neighborhoods or geographic communities.[1] CFW recognized that the ideas and tools for building healthy localities articulated in their work could be applied to organizational settings. On the one hand, the foundation believed the emphasis on discovering and mobilizing internal assets and capacities could provide an appropriate new orientation for nonprofit organizations operating in a universe where traditional avenues of support are contracting. On the other hand, the foundation believed the lessons learned in community settings could not only be applied to organizational settings, but also provide organizations with new ways of understanding themselves as members of the community. Blending these two perspectives provided the underlying framework for the SHOW-21 program.

SHOW-21 is an innovative example of how successful capacity building can be undertaken among nonprofit organizations. More than a program, SHOW-21 is a process that encourages and supports the internalization of an assets focus, the critical exploration of how organizations can more effectively mobilize their many assets and capacities, and the broadening of the relationship base that contributes to organizational sustainability. The SHOW-21 process is based on the assumption that sustainability can be achieved when organizations recognize and understand the full measure of their assets and capacities and then build upon them, generating strong relationships among the internal and external components of the organization's milieu.

CFW recognizes that nonprofit organizations need new and dynamic ways to employ their unique characteristics and strengths in the specific work they do and in partnerships within the larger community. Through SHOW-21, the foundation has successfully:

♦   Defined sustainability as it relates to nonprofits, based on a holistic model that builds on organizational strengths and capacities.

♦   Developed a series of tools for nonprofit organizations to inventory their strengths and weaknesses, their resources, and their needs in order to evaluate their prospects for future sustainability and identify ways to develop components of their asset map that are less mature.

---

[1]   Kretzmann, J. P., & J. L. McKnight (1993). *Building Communities from the Inside Out*. Evanston, IL: Institute for Policy Research, Northwestern University.

♦ Provided technical assistance to participant organizations as they explore the issues, define organizational goals, and implement measures that will increase their sustainability.

♦ Initiated the development of a resource network between nonprofit organizations and the business and corporate community in order to open doors to new relationships and facilitate the provision of technical assistance to ensure the sustainability of the services the organizations offer.

CFW believes that through sharing the SHOW-21 process and the lessons learned it can have a transforming impact on how nonprofits think about their own sustainability and future organizational development. While SHOW-21 was incubated within women's organizations, the process is valuable for the entire nonprofit community. However, because CFW's mission is focused on women, the uniqueness of women's issues, women's assets and capacities, and women's opportunities are at the core of the underlying framework of ideas that supports the SHOW-21 work.

Women's Nonprofit Organizations as a Particular Focus

The SHOW-21 program focused primarily on women's organizations because the foundation believes that an effective model for increasing organizational sustainability might emerge out of recognition of the important differences between women's organizations and other nonprofits. These differences are related to the particular challenges women's organizations have traditionally faced, as well as the unique ways they have approached meeting those challenges. Women's organizations share the underlying assumptions of other nonprofits but also bring a different set of experiences and outlooks to the nonprofit world. These differences can best be viewed through several specific lenses that reflect the uniqueness of women's nonprofits.

The first lens enables us to see how women's organizations play a role in elevating and integrating issues important to women and girls into a broader community agenda. It has been the traditional role of organizations focused on women and girls to lift up these issues by helping to define them as relevant to the entire community and advocating for their incorporation into mainstream thinking. Once this is accomplished, their presence on the agenda opens further opportunities for advocates to shape the community's understanding of related issues and appropriate action. For example, violence against women and girls has been on the women's agenda for the past 25 years, but has only recently become part of broader policy discussions. Because women's organizations stepped in to provide otherwise unavailable services and have advocated over time on the importance of violence as a community problem, the issues have achieved a place on the mainstream agenda. But without the benefit of the knowledge and problem-solving strategies developed by women's organizations, the larger community would have been hard pressed to respond effectively to the problem once it finally recognized its importance. The same argument can be made for other issues traditionally associated with women and girls, including reproductive health care, childcare, and some aspects of economic development.

The second lens reveals the important opportunities women's organizations provide in terms of leadership development and training. Many of the women who are public policy and nonprofit leaders today acquired their leadership abilities through work in women's organizations. The mainstream has provided relatively few opportunities for women to "get their feet wet" and test their leadership skills. The places that can provide safe and supportive environments for such exploration include women's studies programs in our college and university systems and community-based organizations whose voluntary positions are virtually all occupied by women. Women's organizations especially represent an important setting for obtaining and expanding this training.

The third lens reflects the organization itself and its importance in providing a different perspective to the broader nonprofit community. Much like any targeted population that has limited access to traditional power bases, women's organizations provide alternatives—both in terms of what activities they take up and how they manage these endeavors—that represent a powerful contribution to the entire nonprofit community. We know from research that many women seek services from women's organizations rather than from universal programs, and that part of the reason is because they prefer to be treated as unique individuals whose experiences are particular to them. Women's organizations tend to embrace diversity and to generate programs and operational and management styles that take it into account. In doing so, they contribute to the variety of organizational styles necessary to more fully use the talents and skills of all members of society, as well as to address their specific needs.

The SHOW-21 process incorporates and builds on the ways these important differences are manifested in women's organizations. The process also translates what can be learned from these unique experiences into a model that is useful for all nonprofits.

The Importance of "Community" in SHOW-21

CFW recognizes that nonprofit organizations are linked to "community" in complex and multidimensional ways, and has emphasized these important connections in the SHOW-21 program. The traditional role women have played as community leaders is similar to the role they play as leaders of organizations, in part because women are committed to investing in whatever situation or setting they find themselves. Because women's organizations willingly take on addressing the unmet needs associated with tough societal issues, they can themselves be marginalized in terms of the larger community and may occupy community space that is distinct from more mainstream entities. At the same time, the place women's organizations occupy may be seen as central because of the importance of the work they do in the lives of the populations they serve, and the role they play as advocates for social change.

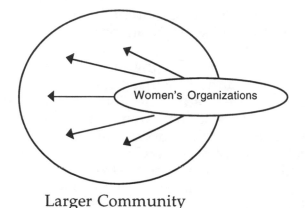

Women's organizations operate at both the center and the margins of the larger community, achieving a powerful influence over mainstream social forces.

Larger Community

In an expanded view of community, nonprofit organizations relate to geographic communities; they are all associated with other communities of constituents, supporters, and funders; and they are typically connected to further communities of related organizations and institutions. While these components of a nonprofit's milieu have not typically been described as "communities," CFW believes that recognizing each element as such allows an organization to tap into the valuable assets existing there and to build stronger relationships with other community members. In terms of the community served or the geographic community, women's organizations already play a crucial role because local women place a high level of trust in them to deliver the services they require. But the geographic community also includes other individuals, organizations, and institutions with which a nonprofit may not have developed relationships, and these represent potential organizational assets. Other aspects of the expanded organizational community—including constituents, supporters, and funders—represent additional assets women's organizations may need to more fully tap into and mobilize. In terms of communities of related organizations and institutions, women's organizations have the potential to share with and influence the activities of these entities, as well as to benefit from the assets they represent. Because this expanded interpretation of community is so appropriate for this work, the SHOW-21 tools are modeled to reflect these various components of an organizational community.

Because women's organizations take responsibility for educating the larger community about the needs of women and girls, and helping to translate important issues into a common language, women's issues *are* community issues. The sustainability of women's organizations is critical if these issues are to remain a salient part of the community agenda. The organizations participating in SHOW-21, for example, contribute to the well-being of Chicago's community of women and girls in multiple ways. Collectively, they provide access to reproductive health education, abortion funding assistance, housing for women in need, substance abuse services, adolescent parenting services, domestic violence programs, violence education, education on older women's needs, research reflecting the needs of low-income persons, education on images of women in the media, opportunities for cultural production, and more. Additionally, they advocate for women and women's rights in local, state, national, and international arenas, and provide opportunities for leadership development. The work they do is critical, and both the individual communities these organizations serve and the Chicago community as a whole benefit when organizations like these maintain a strong sustained presence. SHOW-21 provides a process that can facilitate the building of organizations that can be sustained over time.

Community Reflected in the SHOW-21 Organizational Asset Map

The idea of community is so central to the SHOW-21 work that it forms the framework of the organizational asset map. The organization is envisioned—and the map is constructed—so that the organization itself is the central component. The assets existing in this part of the map include the mission, programs and activities, and accessibility of the organization. Immediately surrounding this component is another layer of assets associated with organization, including human assets and physical, financial, and reputational assets. Finally, an outer layer of assets is comprised of the "community" the organization inhabits. This community is understood in the broadest sense, that is, to include not only the geographic community surrounding the organization, but also organizations and institutions engaged in similar activities, supporters and funders, and the constituency. By envisioning the asset map in this way, the SHOW-21 approach prompts organizations to explore the full range of assets they might be able to tap for capacity-building purposes.

The SHOW-21 Process

The SHOW-21 process was developed and tested over time through a collaborative exploration of ideas and activities, and ongoing group evaluation of process and method. Because the asset-based approach to organizational capacity building assumes that strength and power are generated by broadening and deepening relationships, an important first step in the SHOW-21 process was to bring together a group of individuals capable of working in a collaborative fashion on tough issues and revealing to one another not only their strengths but also their organizational weaknesses and challenges. This first step meant that CFW needed to invest in building a community among the participating organizations in order to **create a highly invested, deeply committed, and trusting working group**. This investment was critical to the success of the SHOW-21 program. Working in a group rather than individually offered each participant not only the benefit of the others' thinking, ideas, and support, but also provided the opportunity for executive directors to remove themselves from the exigencies of program operation and engage in the kind of deep thinking that resulted in the new model for practice. Another key component of the SHOW-21 program was the foundation's investment in **ongoing technical support to the working group**. This was accomplished by hiring a consultant to provide the concepts and methods associated with the assets approach, assist in the process of mapping organizational assets and capacities, facilitate group activities and discussions, guide the development of new definitions, and work with individual participants to develop strategies for mobilizing organizational assets toward increased sustainability. Another critical element in the design of the SHOW-21 program was the fact that the work was accomplished over time with the group coming together on a regular basis to explore issues and develop the model. A short-term process could not have produced the kind of in-depth thinking the **repeated convening of the group** was able to yield. A final element was the **provision of a set of specific challenges** to the group based on the assets approach. These included *developing a definition for organizational sustainability* based on the notion of building on the unique assets and capacities of an organization, *developing self-assessment tools* for organizations to inventory their assets and evaluate their prospects for future sustainability, and *generating a plan* for putting what they learned through asset-mapping into action.

Organizations that Will Benefit From Using the Tools in this Workbook

Although the organizations that participated in the original work presented in this guide were women's organizations, the basic model is appropriate for building the sustainability of any nonprofit organization. In fact, many of the concepts and methods presented here are suitable for *any* organization interested in strengthening itself through the identification and mobilization of its assets. The SHOW-21 approach is primarily one that involves **deep thinking** about the organization within its relational and community settings, **systematic identification**—or mapping—of organizational assets, and **strategic mobilization** of these assets toward increased organizational sustainability.

Because nonprofit organizations have a range of missions defining their activities—as opposed to the relatively narrow purpose of generating profit—increasing their sustainability is both an important and complex undertaking. Many nonprofits have sustained themselves over time by relying on grants from a small base of funders and/or contracts from a few large institutions. In times of plenty, this "traditional" strategy functions well, but in leaner times, organizations may find themselves competing for limited funds and investing large amounts of energy searching for and applying for a reduced set of opportunities. In the process, the organization's focus tends to narrow to finding the money to support the activities defined by the mission. Other important considerations may be left unaddressed and the organization may find itself struggling to remain viable. In women's organizations in particular, a strong commitment to the mission may result in a willingness to accept less than adequate working conditions and compensation in these circumstances, which often leads to burnout and frustration.

The SHOW-21 approach suggests that nonprofits need to comprehensively examine themselves within their organizational settings in order to broaden the focus toward the many assets they possess but which they may not be using to the fullest. By systematically exploring all components of the asset base, an organization can identify potential new ways to generate the financial support it requires. Thus, nonprofit organizations of all sorts can benefit from using the approach presented here. Large or small, engaged in service provision or advocacy, any organization can gain new insights from this model.

<u>Acclaim for SHOW-21 from Program Participants</u>

Recently, the Chicago Foundation for Women posed a series of questions to the organizations in the SHOW-21 working group as a supplement to the ongoing evaluation.

♦   How has the work been used in your organization?

♦   How are you using the asset map?

♦   What changes are happening as a result of your participation?

♦   Have you included anything you learned from your participation in grant writing?

The responses clearly indicate that the experience has been worthwhile for participants and validates CFW's ongoing investment in the work.

♦   Jerri Lynn Fields of **Rape Victim Advocates** (RVA): RVA will use the asset map as a springboard into the strategic planning process. I have asked the board not to rush, but to get ready to jump into the process from the assets perspective. The tools provide a great visible inspiration for our work. I'll be taking a blank map to a staff retreat to really gather their perspective on the organization. The map has helped the board focus on visioning for the organization: Where they want the organization to be and to go emerged from the process of completing the map. From a grant-writing perspective, it's easy to talk about what doesn't work and what's problematic, but now we have a way to focus on what we *can* do, what we're good at, all the positives. It's important to talk about where the organization is going, and the asset map has helped frame the movement toward sustainability. It has also helped us see what we should do with the assets of our board.

♦ Norma Seledón of **Mujeres Latinas en Acción**: I think for Mujeres, the asset map is a validation of things we already knew. For myself personally, going through the process has enabled me to become grounded within the organization. I was a new executive director when I started with SHOW-21, and I've been able to make the shift as new director more easily because of this process. Using the assets perspective throughout is also validating. We have incorporated it into every organizational discussion.

♦ Joan Pikas of **The Enterprising Kitchen** (TEK):: When I heard about SHOW-21 I thought The Enterprising Kitchen might have much to offer to the group, but now I see we have a great deal to learn as well. This approach provides a useful new way to look at the organization. When we started doing the asset-mapping process, I wanted to tear out my hair, but I realized that I was learning a lot about TEK that I hadn't stopped to consider before.

♦ Ann Jenich of **The Enterprising Kitchen** (TEK): TEK just finished a strategic plan using a different model, and we can see it would have been to our advantage to have been able to use the asset map as a base for our planning. We'll use it in the future.

♦ Rebecca Gee of **Women in the Director's Chair** (WIDC): WIDC tends to be asset-based in its perspective, but hasn't traditionally used the language we've learned here. The asset map has been a good visual tool that we have incorporated as a "checkup" on our progress, and one we'll use more in the future. The most important thing about SHOW-21 has been the relationship building we've been able to do. The small group work is great. The language development we've done in the group has helped with grant writing. This assets perspective all comes together very well with the organization's other work.

♦ Jeanne Zimmer of **Housing Opportunities for Women** (HOW): HOW has not taken the asset-mapping process to the board yet, but are planning to do so. When we do, we will explore each category on the organizational map more deeply than we have done so far. HOW did use the map in our strategic-planning process, and adapted it to illustrate our projections for the next five years. It works very well as a visioning tool.

♦ Jenny Knauss of the **Illinois Caucus on Adolescent Health** (ICAH): The map and the process are useful tools. ICAH used the maps and related questions to orient our board members and get them on the same page in terms of their thinking. We are also using them to introduce new board members to the organization. The tools are great because they can be revised and adapted to specific kinds of capacity-building activities within the organization. This work is so important: It would be great if some of our lessons learned could be used to help educate funders about how they can support this kind of effort.

♦ Lisa January of **Older Women's League** (OWL): For the Older Women's League, the asset map provided a visual representation of the organization's spheres of influence and areas of improvement. It was a valuable tool to evaluate the organization's strengths and weaknesses.

♦ Sister Shannon Scallon of **Sisterhouse**: As the incoming executive director of Sisterhouse, the organizational asset map was a very helpful orientation instrument for me. It has also been a useful visual reference tool in working with board members. Our board also found the Mapping Board Member Assets tool very important. The process and the product have given specific focus to board development and they have provided a touchstone for the initial stages of strategic planning. Now much more aware of our strengths, we are all prepared to mobilize them to achieve our goal of long-term sustainability.

THE SHOW-21 EXPERIENCE

THE SHOW-21 EXPERIENCE

The SHOW-21 program was originally designed as a participatory action research project, in which the participants' experiences and learning could be evaluated in an ongoing way and incorporated into the direction in which future activities would proceed. Initial program design identified six goals and a general plan for bringing the organizations together to do the work. Participants themselves quickly took the lead in establishing how the group would interact, how they would reach the six goals, and what specific activities they would undertake in order to do so. Encouraging a flexible approach to the work provided the Chicago Foundation for Women the best opportunity to benefit from the creative thinking of SHOW-21 participants who identified and pursued interim goals as they grappled with the new ways of thinking associated with the program. Encouraging participant ownership of the SHOW-21 program enabled CFW to generate participant commitment to exploring the new approach and developing a new process and tools for increasing organizational sustainability.

Participatory Action Research and Program Evaluation

By implementing a participatory action research and program evaluation mechanism, CFW was able to listen to the SHOW-21 participants and work with them to develop a new approach and the corresponding tools for building organizational sustainability. The primary considerations for the research and evaluation were identified as:

♦   The provision of a supportive environment in which representatives from participating organizations can come up with definitions and criteria for the measurement of success, examine themselves within the framework of those definitions and criteria, and make progress toward implementing ideas toward sustainability.

♦   The development and maintenance of an atmosphere in which representatives from participating organizations can critically evaluate the program, including the contributions of the consultant, the foundation, and the participants.

♦   Flexibility and receptivity on the part of CFW in response to participant activities, output criteria and definitions, and ultimate program goals for each organization.

♦   The comprehensive tracking, recording, and feedback of all program activities; the preparation of materials that illustrate the program's progress and the lessons learned for sharing with other organizations.

♦   The inclusion of multiple voices from within each of the organizations, including the executive director and other SHOW-21 invitees.

♦   The testing of the SHOW-21 model to the outcomes of a parallel interview project among representatives of organizations recently closing their doors as a result of a failure to sustain themselves.

Initial Selection of SHOW-21 Participants

Eight organizations were initially selected by CFW to participate in the SHOW-21 program. The criteria for selection were related to the stability of each organization in terms of its working relationships with others, the organization's status in the larger community, and its financial health. Each selected organization was invited to identify two individuals—the executive director and a member of the board of directors or other representative—for participation in the program. These eight organizations accepted the invitation and participated through the first year or more of the program.

♦   Center for Impact Research (formerly the Taylor Institute)

♦   Chicago Abortion Fund

♦   Housing Opportunities for Women

♦   Illinois Caucus for Adolescent Health

♦   Mujeres Latinas en Acción

♦   Older Women's League of Illinois

♦   Sisterhouse

♦   Women in the Director's Chair

After participation for more than a year, Sisterhouse and the Center for Impact Research modified their involvement in SHOW-21 to participation in a complementary set of activities sponsored by the foundation. Two additional organizations joined the SHOW-21 working group at this time:

♦   Rape Victim Advocates

♦   The Enterprising Kitchen

Promoting Communication Among Participants

In order to build relationships among SHOW-21 participants and encourage ongoing thinking and discourse about issues related to the program, several communication schemes were initiated during year one. Contact information is regularly updated and distributed in order to promote communication among the participants outside of the workshop setting. Micro-cassette recorders were provided to participants for the purpose of developing individual recorded journals whose entries were incorporated into the SHOW-21 record. The taped journal has been used by participants to record relevant ideas and thoughts that arise between workshops, although participants agree that more creative thinking occurs in direct interactions. An electronic listserve discussion site has been discussed as a possibility for linking SHOW-21 participants with each other, with other CFW grantee organizations, and with other nonprofits interested in building sustainability through the assets approach. This idea can be difficult to implement, however, if participants have different levels of technological access and expertise. In general, ongoing opportunities for getting together, getting to know one another, and sharing ideas and experiences represented the best method of promoting communication.

SHOW-21 Workshops and Activities

The activity plan for SHOW-21 included a series of monthly workshops that the executive directors and an additional representative of each organization were invited to attend. Over the first 18 months, participants attended the workshops, explored issues of organizational sustainability, engaged in in-depth asset-mapping activities, and contributed to the development of the tools that represent the heart of this workbook. In addition to the workshops, the activity plan provided for independent meetings between the participants and the SHOW-21 consultant, frequent telephone conversations, and the regular distribution of notes and materials to be added to each individual's ongoing program record. Beyond the workshop activities, in-depth interviews with a small sample of organizations previously funded by CFW but who recently closed their doors were conducted in order to explore why some organizations fail to sustain themselves. CFW compared the findings from these interviews to the definitions of *organizational resiliency* and *organizational sustainability* generated by SHOW-21 participants in order to evaluate the validity of their conclusions about what factors contribute to an organization's ability to withstand major threats and challenges.

As part of the longer-term plan for SHOW-21, CFW has expanded opportunities for exploration of organizational sustainability to the executive directors of all of their grantee organizations through the Executive Director Roundtable program. During these monthly meetings, the foundation has introduced the sustainability concepts, tools, and lessons learned, and provided technical support for organizations wanting to utilize the work more fully within their own organizations. In this way, the foundation is beginning to satisfy the demand for information and support already expressed by other grantees, and both sustain and develop enthusiasm for the highly esteemed work accomplished by first year SHOW-21 participants. The Executive Director Roundtable program has provided opportunities for new SHOW-21 participants to develop organizational asset maps, evaluate their organizations against the definitions developed by the first-year group, and generate their own organizational plans for increasing sustainability. Additionally, new participants benefit from hearing from "experts" from the original working group who facilitate many of the discussions.

At the same time, the original participants have moved on toward implementing specific organizational projects directed at self-identified sustainability objectives. The group continues to come together for workshops on a monthly basis, and works more directly with the SHOW-21 consultant on putting their plans into action.

SHOW-21 Outcomes

The SHOW-21 program has generated a host of outcomes in the form of:

♦   Specific goals achieved

♦   Lessons learned

♦   Relationships promoted

♦   Tools and other products developed

In addition, the foundation has incorporated the theme of mapping and mobilizing organizational assets into many aspects of its work, educating its staff and board members in the concepts and methods associated with the approach. Through their commitment and hard work during the first 18 months of the program, participants have generated a new model of sustainability that may benefit not only their own organizations and others funded by CFW, but also nonprofits everywhere.

Specific Goals Achieved

The first set of outcomes is directly related to the original goals of the SHOW-21 program. In this section, the goals are revisited and the specific outcomes related to each goal are stressed.

SHOW-21 GOAL #1: Defining sustainability as it relates to women's organizations, based on a holistic model that builds on women's unique strengths and capacities.

Through a process of ongoing discussion and deliberation, SHOW-21 participants produced a definition for sustainability that relies on a two-part understanding of the term. The first part of the definition is called *resiliency*, and the second part is called *sustainability*. The terms are understood in relationship to one another, with each part representing a position along a continuum conceptualized as *organizational sustainability*, and the term sustainability occupying a position further along the continuum than resiliency. In addition, the definition for resiliency suggests a more reactive than proactive organizational mode, that is, resiliency means an organization is able to effectively respond to the various situations it encounters. The definition for sustainability, on the other hand, suggests more ability on the part of the organization to be proactive about using its strengths to its best advantage, rather than only responding to external pressures and opportunities.[2]

> **SHOW-21 GOAL #2**: Developing self-assessment tools for women's organizations to inventory their strengths and weaknesses, their resources, and their needs in order to evaluate their prospects for future sustainability and identify ways to build components of the asset map that are less mature.

Although the SHOW-21 Tool Box will be expanded on an ongoing basis, it currently consists of 12 organizational assessment activities and tools. Each tool is used either independently or collectively with other organizations. However, because of the enormous value to be gained through collaborative work on these issues, the Chicago Foundation for Women recommends using the tools in group settings. In this way, the sharing of ideas enables participants to expand their own thinking, to apply the experience of other organizations to their own setting, and to develop lasting supportive relationships within a new "community" of related organizations. The current SHOW-21 Tool Box includes 12 tools:

♦ Convening an Organizational Sustainability Working Group

♦ Mapping Organizational Assets

♦ Exploring Organizational Resiliency

♦ Thinking Out of the Box—Mobilizing Organizational Assets

♦ Exploring Organizational Sustainability

♦ Mapping Employee Assets

♦ Mapping Board Member Assets

♦ Mapping Volunteer Assets

♦ Mapping Constituent Assets

♦ Mapping Who We Know—Six Degrees of Separation

♦ Mapping Our Stories—How We Articulate Our Organizational Strengths

♦ Mapping What the Organization has to Offer Toward Creating Board Diversity

---

[2] The definitions for organizational resiliency and organizational sustainability are included in the SHOW-21 tools *Exploring Organizational Resiliency* and *Exploring Organizational Sustainability* in the Chapter titled *The SHOW-21 Tool Box*.

Each tool is presented in the form of an "Asset Map" and includes a description, a set of goals, and a set of learning concepts, as well as examples of how the particular map or exercise has been used in a real-life setting. Each tool is presented in a way that emphasizes a Group Activity, a more in-depth Organizational Activity, and a Tailored Organizational Activity suitable for modification for specific settings. Each tool provides a blank worksheet for use by the organization or working group, as well as an example of a completed worksheet. The example worksheets each represent the experience of a single organization or, in a few cases, a compilation of activities engaged in by several organizations. Many tools provide a set of questions designed to facilitate exploration of a specific topic or component of the asset map in question. These mapping tools can be modified to suit each organization's specific program design.

> **SHOW-21 GOAL #3**: Providing technical assistance to SHOW-21 participant organizations as they explore the issues, define organizational goals, and implement measures that will increase their sustainability.

The SHOW-21 program was designed to provide several kinds of technical assistance. Participants in the original working group have had access to the time of the SHOW-21 consultant, both through the workshop activities and through individual meetings. Ongoing technical support is available for developing and modifying the organizational asset maps, and for individual participants who have taken the initiative to translate the tools into organization-specific devices for independent asset-building work.

> **SHOW-21 GOAL #4**: Initiating the development of a resource network between women's organizations and the business and corporate community in order to open doors to new relationships and facilitate the provision of technical assistance to women's nonprofits to ensure the sustainability of the services they offer to women and girls.

One important aspect of the SHOW-21 program was the willingness of the Chicago Foundation for Women to be a supporting partner to the participating organizations. As the work progressed and participants identified ways they could benefit from expanded networks, the foundation stepped forward to bring its extensive resources into the process. This took the form of inviting representatives of the local business and corporate communities to address the group on topics of interest, promoting more interaction between SHOW-21 participants and members of the foundation's Businesswomen's Leadership Council, and organizing a technology advisory committee capable of educating SHOW-21 participants about appropriate and necessary technology and assisting them to bring their organizations up to speed. For organizations considering something like the SHOW-21 program, working with a supportive partner such as a foundation can facilitate the implementation of program learning through expanded access to even more communities where specific kinds of expertise can be found.

> **SHOW-21 GOAL #5**: Evaluating the SHOW-21 process with the intention of making models and tools available to women's organizations and general service organizations for the planning and development of sustainable community-based services for women and girls.

The ongoing participatory action research and program evaluation component of SHOW-21 has resulted in several comprehensive reports which explain the process and outcomes of the program, provide examples of the activities undertaken by participating organizations, and present early versions of the model and tools developed. This workbook represents the culmination of efforts to make the information available to women's organizations and other nonprofits.

> **SHOW-21 GOAL # 6**: Exploring the risks and challenges specific to women's organizations, and gathering stories from organizations that have not survived.

As part of the SHOW-21 program, representatives of organizations that were previously funded by CFW but which recently closed their doors were identified for participation in an interview project. The SHOW-21 planning team developed a survey for these organizations to help identify patterns, similarities, and differences among organizations unable to survive in order to allow other organizations to learn from their experiences. The interviews explored questions similar to those examined in the organizational asset-mapping process used by SHOW-21 participants, but focused on the reasons for the organization's failure to thrive (i.e., in what ways organizational assets were insufficient or inadequately mobilized, and in what ways the situation led to the organization's closure). The information gathered through these interviews has been used to test the characteristics of sustainability developed by participating organizations and incorporated into the definition.

As part of the exploration of former organizations, representatives from nine groups were contacted and interviewed. Their responses to questions in the areas of strategic planning, board of directors, mission, resources, programming, staff, and issues related to the prevention of closing provided key insights in the area of organizational sustainability. Factors implicated in the closures included the following:

♦ Lack of strategic planning was an issue for about half of the organizations; four of the nine organizations did not have a strategic plan in place.

♦ Most of the organizations interviewed indicated problems between members of the board and the executive director or staff by the time the organization was about to dissolve.

♦ All the organizations indicated that their board members brought important capacities to their work—including expertise in the service area, commitment to the cause or mission, diversity, and involvement in fundraising—but notably absent from the list was the capacity to help the organization achieve sustainability or to help it recover from a problematic situation.

♦ All of the closed organizations had a volunteer Board of Directors; for many there were no term limits or term limits that were either unenforced or only loosely enforced.

♦ Two organizations reported serious problems with financial accounting: In one case no audit was available for the previous year and in another case the board was given inaccurate financial information by a former executive director and comptroller.

♦ Two closed organizations reported the organization had no clear mission; others were operating with only a vague mission statement.

♦ Fund raising was a problem for most of the organizations, mainly due to insufficient staff to pursue appropriate funding.

♦ Most of the organizations indicated that they had no earned income; many had limited diversity in their funding streams.

♦ Most of the organizations had problems with finding and keeping adequate staff.

In the final analysis, these organizations closed due to their being insufficiently aware of or engaged in all the aspects of their organization's capacity building, and their failure to maintain strong ties with all aspects of their multidimensional "community." Most had been floundering for some time but had not sought help from outside; most thought they could get through the crisis without having a sense of what needed to be in place in order to maintain their sustainability.

Lessons Learned

In addition to the definitions and tools developed, the work done by participants in SHOW-21 has resulted in a number of lessons learned. The following list illustrates some examples.

Definitional Aspects of Lessons Learned

♦   Sustainability is directly related to the extent to which an organization is able to mobilize its assets toward generating the ongoing resources necessary to maintain its mission and carry out high-quality work.

♦   The sustainability of organizations that consider themselves progressive, feminist agents for social change is also related to their adherence to a set of guiding principles that reflect certain kinds of values, commitments, and methods of carrying out the organizational mission.   For example, organizations committed to working on such issues as living wage or equal access to health care must incorporate those ideals into their own operations. Poverty wages and inadequate benefits will not attract the kind of employee that can contribute to an organization's sustainability.

♦   Sustainability incorporates the qualities of resiliency, or the extent to which an organization is able to carry out its mission in situations of adversity, and to respond to and manage planned and unplanned change or new opportunities.

♦   Sustainability depends on integrating multiple voices into organizational strategizing, planning, and program implementation; the most appropriate voices are often those of people already affiliated in some way—as constituents, board members, staff, or collaborators—rather than outside experts.

♦   Sustainability assumes certain abilities on the part of organizational representatives—to respond quickly and effectively to threats and challenges, to be flexible and open to new ways of doing things, to be proactive and ready to pursue new opportunities.

Lessons Learned About Asset Mapping and Mobilizing

♦   The work of asset mapping and mobilizing assets toward increased organizational sustainability can be enhanced through building a community with which to share the exploration. A supportive community provides a space in which ideas can be shared, more learning takes place, confidence in the ability to succeed is generated, and resources to meet organizational needs may be available.

♦   The work of mapping and mobilizing organizational assets depends to some extent on having time in which to get away from the daily tasks of the organization, to think deeply, explore, plan, and allow creativity to flow.

♦   More effective asset mobilization can occur if an organization first:

   ↳ Engages in asset mapping in more depth among different individuals related to the organization, such as staff, board members, constituency, or volunteers. Explores the assets identified and how other opportunities might be provided for these individuals to contribute more of what they have to offer.

> ℀ Engages in asset mapping in more depth among the larger community of individuals, organizations, and institutions with whom the organization is related. Explores the assets identified and the possibility of mutually beneficial expansions of these relationships, and the development of new relationships.

> ℀ Identifies the various forms of expertise possessed by the organization in any one of its components, and explores the possibilities for generating income through the marketing of this expertise. Specific ideas include: generating earned income through admission to activities and events, and through rental fees; charging a small fee for information currently distributed for free; initiating a sliding-scale fee for services; charging a consulting fee for speaker services.

> ℀ Identifies opportunities for reducing organizational expenditures, for example, through the sharing of space, employees, consultants, equipment, transportation, bulk material purchases, knowledge, and expertise with other organizations in the geographic vicinity.

◆ Many nonprofits have gaps in their organizational asset maps, particularly in their relationships to the business and corporate worlds and other entities not normally associated with the nonprofit sector. Filling these gaps may depend on willingness to fundamentally change organizational thinking and expose certain myths (e.g., adopting effective business practices is not the equivalent of adopting a profit motive).

◆ When building an organization from the assets approach, it is important to always look within or nearby first, as developing a resource that already exists is more productive than nurturing an entirely new one.

◆ Most nonprofits already have relationships with individuals who could facilitate the development of new relationships with business and corporate entities; these individuals represent an untapped asset for many organizations.

Other Lessons Learned

◆ Women's organizations are uniquely positioned to increase their sustainability through asset mapping and mobilizing methods because women tend to approach their activities with open communication, and in a less hierarchical and more cooperative manner.

◆ When committed people come together around a common goal or purpose, their power to generate new ideas is increased exponentially.

◆ Organizations previously funded by CFW but that have recently closed their doors, would have rated low on most of the characteristics of sustainability identified by SHOW-21 participants.

◆ Closed organizations were especially weak in their level of connectedness to other organizations; increasing isolation was common as they approached dissolution; most did not share their difficulties with others who might have been able to offer assistance in holding the organization together or facilitating its transformation into something more sustainable.

◆ Having a convener to sponsor the activities of an organizational sustainability working group is advantageous because this entity can support the workshops in terms of space and materials for meetings, provide assistance with identifying and compensating a consultant or other facilitator, make connections to specific kinds of expertise the group may require, and promote the work in larger circles.

Relationships Promoted

Although most of the participating organizations reported having connections with other organizations and institutions through various collaborative activities prior to their entering the SHOW-21 program, their involvement has produced some positive outcomes in this regard. At the end of the first year of the program, the participants all agree that one of the most important outcomes of the program has been the relationships they have developed with the other participants. The opportunity provided by CFW to come together on a regular basis in a supportive and confidential setting has allowed SHOW-21 participants to:

◆ Build a high level of trust among members of the group.

◆ Share both problems and organizational success in a non-judgmental atmosphere where support and encouragement are always provided.

◆ Try out new ideas among friends who share a willingness to be challenged to evolve fresh ways of thinking.

◆ Develop a sense of cohesiveness and membership in a group of supportive women with similar commitments.

SHOW-21 participants anticipate that the relationships they have developed through their work in the program will be lasting ones, and that they will be able to call on these new friends for support and ideas in the future.

In addition to these strong relationships, participants have developed a new sense of the importance other organizational relationships may have in their future sustainability. Through the process of developing the organizational asset maps, each participant has examined the extensiveness of her current networks, and has identified areas in which current relationships could be strengthened, or new ones developed. One of the special characteristics of women's organizations is their unique capacity for connectedness, for being a member of a strong community of organizations working together. However, one of the discoveries of the SHOW-21 program demonstrates that although women's organizations may have the natural capacity for collaboration and connectedness, the fact that many tend to operate in crisis mode a great deal of the time may interfere with their membership in some of these groups. In other words, what may be a fairly standard operating mode can result in isolation that further reduces an organization's sustainability. Having explored this question as a group, SHOW-21 participants have a heightened awareness of the importance of maintaining strong connections with individuals and entities in every component of their asset map.

Tools and Other Products Developed

The following chapter and remainder of this workbook share the tools and other products developed by the SHOW-21 program. An initial set of 12 organization-building tools are included here, as well as instructions for various ways to use them. The definitions developed by SHOW-21 participants for organizational resiliency and organizational sustainability are incorporated into two tools that provide the opportunity to explore any organization against the definitions.

THE SHOW-21 TOOL BOX

THE SHOW-21 TOOL BOX

As a result of the success of the SHOW-21 program, the Chicago Foundation for Women is able to recommend and provide tools that may be used for the replication of this effort and its outcomes in other settings. Each tool reflects an activity designed to move an organization through the exploration of a specific set of goals and learning concepts. Each tool has been developed through the work of the SHOW-21 participants, and represents what the group considers an effective guide for other organizations as they explore issues of sustainability.

The Value of Working in a Group

For any organization interested in exploring issues of sustainability, other organizations that share an affinity can represent a powerful and potentially supportive community. This "community" of organizations is important for both the success of the process and the nurturing of organizational efforts to increase sustainability. In terms of the process itself, having the benefit of different perspectives and different experiences results in much greater learning for each individual organization. Additionally, one of the important lessons learned through SHOW-21 was that sustainability is positively influenced by strong connections to other organizations. Much of the work of mobilizing organizational assets and building organizational capacity toward sustainability depends on the network of relationships the organization cultivates. We therefore encourage several organizations to join together and form a *working group* through which to conduct this work.

In the process of organizing an organizational sustainability working group, it is important to think about who the appropriate convener of such a group might be. In the case of SHOW-21, the convener was the Chicago Foundation for Women, a funder of each of the participating groups. The advantages of having a funder convene the organizations include the funder's ability to support the workshops in terms of space and materials for meetings, assistance with identifying and compensating a consultant or other facilitator, connections to specific kinds of expertise the group may require, and the ability to promote the work in larger circles. Others might also convene such a group; the possibilities include (a) a neighborhood-based organization, (b) a community development corporation, (c) a local institution such as a library or school, (d) a coalition of nonprofit organizations, or (e) a group of individuals representing nonprofit organizations interested in the work. In fact, anyone interested in supporting and promoting the health of local nonprofit organizations might act as the convener. Some entities will clearly be in a position to provide more financial and material support than others, and this support can be an important part of allowing participants the time necessary to do the critical work of building organizational sustainability.

Design of the SHOW-21 Tools

Each tool is designed so that the first part of the activity is conducted within a multi-organizational working group followed by a more in-depth exploration of the issues within each individual organization. CFW also recognizes that individual organizations and working groups may benefit from tailoring the tools to fit a specific setting or situation. As a result, the tools are formulated as multi-purpose instruments that both reflect the specific process engaged in by the SHOW-21 participants and provide flexibility to others interested in making them more relevant to their own setting. Each tool is therefore presented in its original form and in an adaptable version, and an example of a completed version of each tool is provided.[3] Instructions are provided for each tool under the headings *Group Activity* and *Organizational Activity*; these reflect the process as designed by the original SHOW-21 working group. Additionally, instructions are provided under the heading *Tailored Organizational Activity*; these provide the opportunity for site-specific modification. Finally, under the heading *Applications*, an example or set of examples are provided to illustrate how the tool has been used in a real-life setting.

Using the Tools in Order

These tools are organized in a series and the activities included in them will probably have the greatest impact if they are undertaken in the order in which they are presented. Each tool is designed to build upon the knowledge gained in the tools preceding it; the learning is cumulative and we suggest the adoption of the entire process, if possible, rather than the independent use of individual tools.

The SHOW-21 Tool Box includes:

♦ **Convening an Organizational Sustainability Working Group**: This activity identifies potential conveners and challenges the convener to identify appropriate members for a working group that will come together regularly to explore issues of sustainability.

♦ **Mapping Organizational Assets**: This tool takes an organization through a process of in-depth self-examination and identification of internal and external assets that are available to be mobilized toward increased organizational sustainability. The tool provides a system of graphic representation of the assets identified, as well as a set of questions designed to guide the process.

♦ **Exploring Organizational Resiliency**: This activity requires the organization to "test" itself against a multi-dimensional definition of organizational resiliency. The original SHOW-21 working group identified resiliency as an important precursor to organizational sustainability and developed a list of

---

[3] In cases where a completed worksheet example uses the name of an individual, names have been changed. In the Application section of each tool, names of real organizations are often used.

characteristics of this condition that comprise the definition. The tool requires frank assessment of the strengths of the organization, and a willingness to examine areas in which improvements could be made.

♦ **Thinking Out of the Box—Mobilizing Organizational Assets**: This series of exercises is designed to help participants break out of their standard ways of thinking about organizational development, eliminate artificial constraints on their creativity, identify new ways of meeting challenges and opportunities, and begin to examine previously unexplored ways of mobilizing assets toward organizational sustainability.

♦ **Exploring Organizational Sustainability**: This exercise requires the organization to "test" itself against a multi-dimensional definition of organizational sustainability developed by the original SHOW-21 working group. It requires frank assessment of the current status of the organization and a willingness to explore areas in which improvements could be made.

♦ **Mapping Employee Assets**: This tool challenges the organization to think about each individual employee and develop a more complete view of who the employee really is, identify what the employee would most like to be doing for the organization and what responsibilities would make the most of their capacities, and expand the avenues for contribution to the organization based on what each employee brings to the table.

♦ **Mapping Board Member Assets**: This exercise provides the opportunity for the organization to think about each board member and develop a more comprehensive view of the individual, discover what kind of contribution each one would most like to make to the organization, analyze what responsibilities would make the most of their capacities, and expand the avenues for contribution to the organization based on what each individual brings to the table.

♦ **Mapping Volunteer Assets**: This activity asks the organization to think about each volunteer and develop a more complete view of who the individual really is, identify what they would most like to do for the organization, and expand the avenues for contribution to the organization based on what each volunteer brings to the table.

♦ **Mapping Constituent Assets**: This tool challenges the organization to think about its constituents and develop a more comprehensive view of the groups and individuals who fit into this category, identify how they might be developed as a more integral part of the organization, and expand avenues for contribution to the organization for the members of this varied group.

♦ **Mapping Who We Know—Six Degrees of Separation**: This tool uses the notion of "Six Degrees of Separation" to examine the complexity of the web of relationships of the organization's board members or any other organizational grouping. In our example, it is used as a the basis of a fund-raising activity.

♦   **Mapping Our Stories—How We Articulate Our Organizational Strengths**: This tool helps the organization and its board members or any other organizational grouping develop a way of thinking about and articulating the strengths of the organization through stories.

♦   **Mapping What the Organization has to Offer Toward Creating Board Diversity**: This tool helps the organization identify what opportunities they can offer to attract potential new board members. Candidates from diverse backgrounds may be attracted by different aspects of how participation can enhance their lives.

The remainder of the SHOW-21 Tool Box section of this workbook is organized around the specific tools. Each tool begins with a statement of the goals of the exercise and the learning concepts associated with the tool. Most tools include one or two worksheets that will facilitate completion of the exercise. Where appropriate, both the worksheets developed by the original SHOW-21 working group and a version designed for individual tailoring are included. The original worksheets are headed with the worksheet title and the subtitle *SHOW-21 Version*. The worksheets designed for tailoring are headed with the same worksheet title but indicate *Tailored Activity Version* in the subtitle. Within the text of each tool, both SHOW-21 and Tailored Activity Versions are referred to in **bold face type**.

CONVENING AN ORGANIZATIONAL SUSTAINABILITY WORKING GROUP

GOALS ☞

The Goals of this Exercise are:

♦ To identify organizations that share a geographic location, an organizational mission, a style of operations, a common funder, or other affinity.

♦ To assess the likelihood of these organizations' receptiveness to the idea of participating in an organizational sustainability working group.

♦ To generate a list of organizations to invite to participate.

LEARNING
CONCEPTS ☞

The Learning Concepts Associated with this Exercise are:

♦ *Organizational Sustainability Working Group*—the benefit to all participants that will result from working as a group to explore issues of organizational sustainability using the SHOW-21 model.

♦ *Organizational Affinities*—how to select other organizations with which to form a working group based on the characteristics of both groups.

This exercise provides an opportunity to identify a group of organizations with which it might be possible to form an organizational sustainability working group. A working group should be comprised of representatives of organizations who can collectively explore issues related to sustainability. Its members should share some kind of organizational affinity, whether it is one of mutual respect, related mission, similar circumstances, or geographic vicinity. The main purpose of forming a working group is to assure the greatest possible benefit from using the SHOW-21 tools. The working group provides a safe environment in which to explore challenging questions, a supportive network of colleagues who can provide valuable feedback for each participant's experiences and ideas and contribute expertise to developing plans, and a source from which each participant will undoubtedly learn about new resources that may benefit her organization.

GROUP OR ORGANIZATIONAL ACTIVITY

This is a preliminary exercise and may be completed by a potential convener—that is, a sponsor of the newly formed organizational sustainability working group—or by one or two other organizations that are interested in the process and trying to identify other organizations to participate. Ideally, a working group should meet together every month or so to work through the exercises in the SHOW-21 Tool Box. Between meetings, participants can expand the learning by working through the assigned exercise in more depth within their own organization. Returning to the group the following month to share these in-depth lessons adds value for every participant. An organizational sustainability working group can form on its own, but having a convener that takes on a supportive role is an advantage. A convener might be (a) a funder, (b) a neighborhood-based organization, (c) a community development corporation, (d) a local institution such as a library or school, (e) a coalition of nonprofit organizations, or (e) a group of individuals representing nonprofit organizations interested in the work. A convener in the position to provide some degree of financial and material support would be ideal. In cases where a working group is impossible, the SHOW-21 tools can be used independently within a single organization.

In this exercise, users should creatively examine the kinds of affinities they might have with other groups, and examine what advantages different groups might gain from working together. Using the following questions as a guide, identify four to eight other organizations that might be able to come together in an organizational sustainability working group to implement the SHOW-21 process.

FIRST, CONSTRUCT A LIST OF POSSIBLE ORGANIZATIONS:

1. What organizations in the general geographic vicinity are dealing with similar issues?

2. What organizations exist in the vicinity that already have some kind of working relationship?

3. What organizations share the same, similar, or related missions?

4. What organizations share a similar style of operations?

5. What organizations have executive directors with excellent reputations or for whom people have great respect?

6. What organizations in the vicinity generate a high level of respect in terms of their operations, their mission, their history, their successes, etc.?

NEXT, EXAMINE EACH ACCORDING TO THE FOLLOWING QUESTIONS:

1. Of all the organizations listed in response to the first seven questions, which are relatively stable and ready to explore issues related to increasing organizational sustainability?

2. Of all the organizations listed, which might be able to entertain new ideas and new ways of thinking about building sustainability through the mobilization of their assets?

3. Which of these organizations could develop strong and meaningful connections through a working relationship designed around the exploration of organizational assets?

4. Which of these organizations might be able to devote several hours of time per month of the executive director, president, CEO, etc. to a collaborative exploration of these issues?

FINALLY, INVITE ORGANIZATIONS TO JOIN AN ORGANIZATIONAL SUSTAINABILITY WORKING GROUP:

Between four and eight other organizations are probably ideal for a working group. Fewer than four may not provide the range of experiences and expertise that will facilitate collective growth. More than eight may mean that the group encounters difficulties in scheduling meetings and that there is an insufficient amount of time for individual participants to share their ideas. If four to eight can be identified, invite them to participate. If a convener has undertaken the use of this tool, be prepared to describe to invitees the responsibilities you plan to assume in relationship to the working group, as well as the expectations. If a group of organizations has undertaken the use of this tool, be prepared to describe to invitees the expectations of group participation. If the convener can provide, or the working group is able to obtain, the services of a facilitator who is familiar with the SHOW-21 model, the process of working through the tools will be more productive.

If an organization is interested in using the SHOW-21 tools independently or is unable to identify other organizations interested in working together, the tools may be used by a single organization. In this case, it would still be to the advantage of the organization to obtain the services of a facilitator able to assist with the process of using the tools internally. For example, the facilitator could lead board members or staff in the development of an organizational asset map, and could lead discussions among board members about the mobilization of the organizational assets identified through the mapping process.

APPLICATION

Example 1:

The Chicago Foundation for Women convened an organizational sustainability working group by identifying eight organizations from among its grantees who came together on a long-term basis and engaged in the work that resulted in this workbook. The foundation supported the working group by offering a small stipend for participation to each executive director; providing space, materials, and refreshments in support of the regular meetings; designating staff time to administrative tasks associated with the work; and compensating a SHOW-21 consultant/facilitator for time invested in working with the group members and writing a program report.

Example 2:

A suburban foundation in Illinois convened a short-term organizational sustainability working group by offering a set of eight workshops centered around the SHOW-21 work to their grantee organizations at a modest cost. Forty organizations took advantage of the opportunity; the foundation subsidized the cost of the workshops and the time of facilitators who conducted the workshops.

Example 3:

A nonprofit organization based in Illinois used the SHOW-21 tools in an internal capacity-building effort. The group obtained the services of a SHOW-21 facilitator who guided members of the board of directors through a day-long series of asset mapping and mobilizing exercises. Their work was used to develop a strategic plan and redirect the activities of the organization.

MAPPING ORGANIZATIONAL ASSETS

GOALS ☞

> **The Goals of this Exercise are:**
>
> ◆ To systematically examine the various components of the organization and the relationships between and among them.
>
> ◆ To generate a visual and text-based map of the organization's assets and capacities including those present in its relationship network.
>
> ◆ To develop a deeper understanding of the organization within its milieu.
>
> ◆ To prepare for the deeper work of exploring organizational sustainability.

LEARNING
CONCEPTS ☞

> **The Learning Concepts Associated with this Exercise are:**
>
> ◆ *Assets and Capacities*—the importance of shifting the emphasis of organizational thinking from needs and deficiencies to assets and capacities.
>
> ◆ *Mapping*—the systematic exploration of organizational assets and capacities and the role of mapping in creating and institution-alizing this shift.
>
> ◆ *Mobilizing*—the deliberate utilization of assets and capacities in every aspect of organizational activity.
>
> ◆ *Asset Map*—the visual and text-based tool illustrating the assets and capacities upon which the organization may draw in its efforts to increase sustainability.

The first—and most critical—step in building organizational sustainability is to explore the organization from the assets perspective. This means that a new way of thinking must be adopted, one that moves away from evaluating the needs and deficiencies of the organization and toward viewing it in terms of its assets. Although most of those in leadership positions would contend that they are already aware of the many positive aspects of their organizations, this exercise will help to fine tune the ability to really focus on organizational assets in ways that will reveal how many there really are, and show how to understand them in ways that can lead to increased sustainability. Through a process of systematic identification—or mapping—of these assets, the organization can develop both visual and text-based versions of the resulting information. This product is called an organizational asset map, and it functions as a tool through which the organization can strategically plan the mobilization of its assets toward increased sustainability.

GROUP ACTIVITY

The initial asset-mapping experience can take place in the organizational sustainability working group. Each participant should use a blank copy of the **Organizational Asset Map (SHOW-21 Version)** included at the end of this tool for the exercise. Group members should spend about 20 minutes thinking independently and filling in the boxes on the worksheet. At the end of this period, participants should share with the group something about the specific organizational assets they were able to identify in each category. A discussion can then occur among the group members about the kinds of things participants included on their asset map. The discussion should spark new ideas for everyone about what kinds of things may be viewed as assets.

ORGANIZATIONAL ACTIVITY

The completion of the final asset map should be accomplished as an internal activity within each organization. Each working group participant should invite others within their own organization to assist in the process. These individuals may be selected from among members of the board, employees, or committee members, and should include whoever is deemed an important part of the organization's development. The goals are to explore and understand the organization within its entire milieu, to generate a visual and text-based map of the organization's assets and capacities, and to prepare for further exploration of organizational sustainability. The following questions should be used as a guide for exploring the organization's assets and capacities in an in-depth manner. The written answers to the questions form the text-based asset map; when transferred to the appropriate boxes of the **Organizational Asset Map (SHOW-21 version)**, a visual version is produced. Once each organization has completed a visual and text version of the asset map, the working group can come together again to learn about other participating organizations and begin to share ideas about utilizing assets to the fullest.

ASSET-MAPPING QUESTIONS

A.   THE ORGANIZATION ITSELF:

1.   What is the mission of the organization?

2.   What programs, events, and activities does the organization provide?

3.   Where is the organization located?

4.   Is the organization accessible to employees, board members, and constituency? In what ways is the location an asset?

B.   THE HUMAN ASSETS:

1.   Who are the employees and what capacities do they possess?

2.   What do you know about the capacities of your employees beyond the obvious ones they bring to their work with you?

3.   Who are the board members and what capacities do they possess?

4.   What do you know about the capacities of your board members beyond the obvious ones they bring to their work with you?

5.   Who are the volunteers and what capacities do they possess?

6.   What do you know about the capacities of your volunteers beyond the obvious ones they bring to their work with you?

C.   THE PHYSICAL/FINANCIAL/REPUTATIONAL ASSETS:

1.   What are the physical assets of the organization (e.g., space, equipment, and materials)?

2.   What are the financial assets of the organization?

3.   What are the organization's current funding sources?

4.   Are these sources diverse and do they provide multi-year funding?

5.   What is the reputation of the organization in the community?

D.   THE CONSTITUENCY:

1.   Who are the individuals the organization currently serves?

2.   What do you know about the capacities of your constituents beyond the obvious ones they bring to their participation in your programs, events, and activities?

3. In what ways do you currently take advantage of the capacities of individuals you serve or have served in the past?

E. COMMUNITY OF RELATED ORGANIZATIONS AND INSTITUTIONS:

1. To what extent is the organization connected to other organizations and institutions with common goals?

2. What do you know about the capacities of these related organizations and institutions beyond the obvious ones they bring to their current relationships with the organization?

3. What is the nature of these relationships in terms of the specific things they enable the organization to accomplish?

F. THE COMMUNITY OF GEOGRAPHIC ORGANIZATIONS AND INSTITUTIONS:

1. To what extent is the organization connected to other organizations and institutions within its own geographic community?

2. What do you know about the assets and capacities of any of these organizations or institutions?

3. What is the nature of these relationships in terms of the specific things they enable the organization to accomplish?

4. To what extent do the missions or agendas of these organizations overlap?

G. THE SUPPORTERS AND FUNDERS:

1. What kinds of relationships does the organization have with its various supporters and funders?

2. What do you know about the assets and capacities of any of these supporters and funders?

3. What is the nature of these relationships in terms of the specific things they enable the organization to accomplish beyond the funds they provide?

TAILORED ORGANIZATIONAL ACTIVITY

The completion of the final asset map is probably best accomplished by tailoring the asset-mapping process to each specific organization. Inevitably, the categories designed for the participants in one kind of working group may be inappropriate for another working group. Similarly, the categories designed for a particular organization may not provide for an adequate exploration of another organization. Therefore, each organization is encouraged to make whatever modifications seem appropriate in order to make the most of the asset-mapping process. A completely blank **Organizational Asset Map (Tailored Activity Version)** suitable for modifying is provided for a more individualized approach to the activity. With this version of the map, each organization can select the categories that best describe its own organizational and community milieus and enter them as headings on the blank map. The guiding questions can then be adjusted to reflect the new headings. Tailored maps also represent a valuable learning tool and can be shared with the larger working group.

APPLICATION

Example 1:

The participating organizations in the SHOW-21 program each completed an organizational asset map using the categories in the **SHOW-21 Version**. Several of the participants then advanced the work within their own organizations by renaming and adding categories within the various layers of asset components so that they were able to capture the wide range of assets potentially available to them.

Example 2:

A group of organizations working together on the SHOW-21 sustainability process used the **Tailored Activity Version** as the basis from which to build an exercise that would enable them to capture each of their assets in a specific part of the map. By renaming every "box" on the worksheet, assets were organized into categories that made sense to the group.

ORGANIZATIONAL ASSET MAP

SHOW-21 VERSION

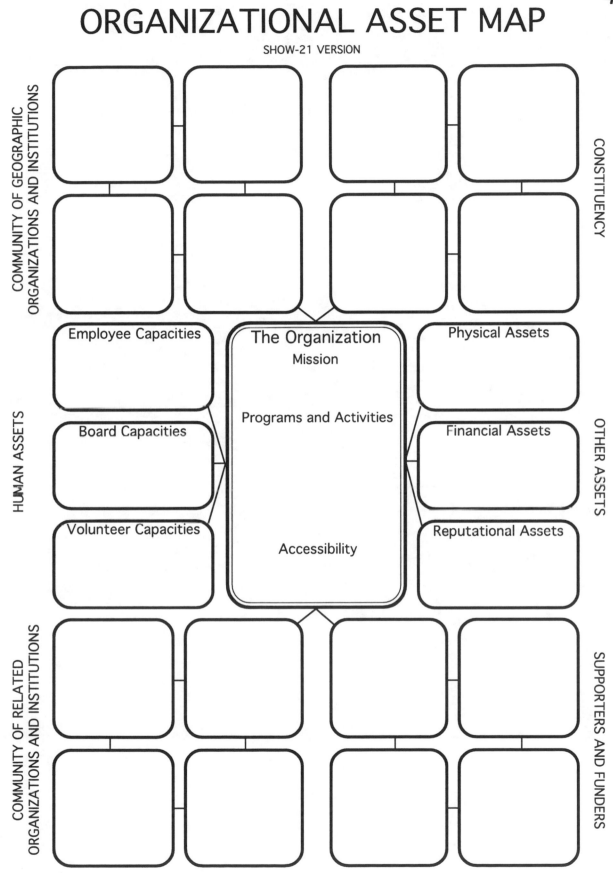

COMMUNITY OF GEOGRAPHIC ORGANIZATIONS AND INSTITUTIONS

CONSTITUENCY

HUMAN ASSETS

OTHER ASSETS

COMMUNITY OF RELATED ORGANIZATIONS AND INSTITUTIONS

SUPPORTERS AND FUNDERS

Employee Capacities

Board Capacities

Volunteer Capacities

The Organization

Mission

Programs and Activities

Accessibility

Physical Assets

Financial Assets

Reputational Assets

43

ORGANIZATIONAL ASSET MAP

TAILORED ACTIVITY VERSION

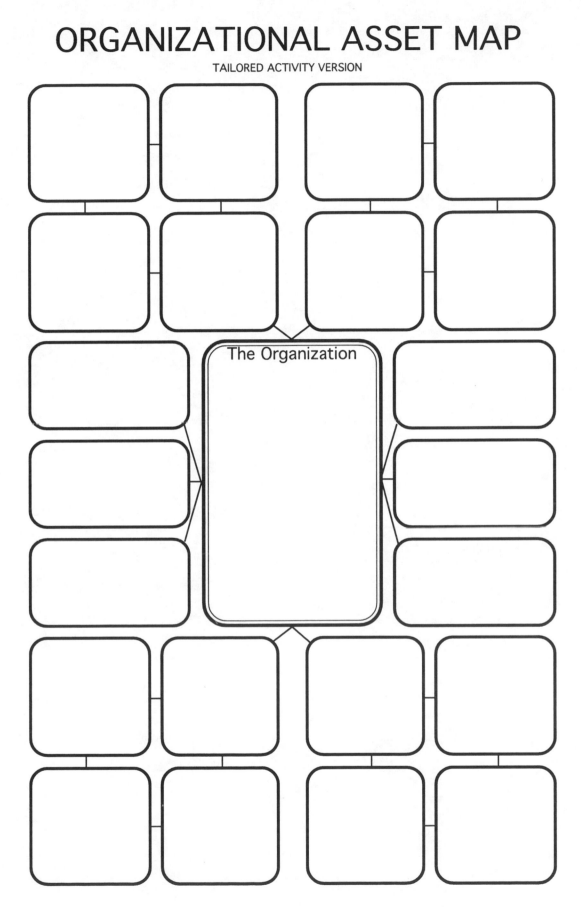

The Organization

ORGANIZATIONAL ASSET MAP

EXAMPLE

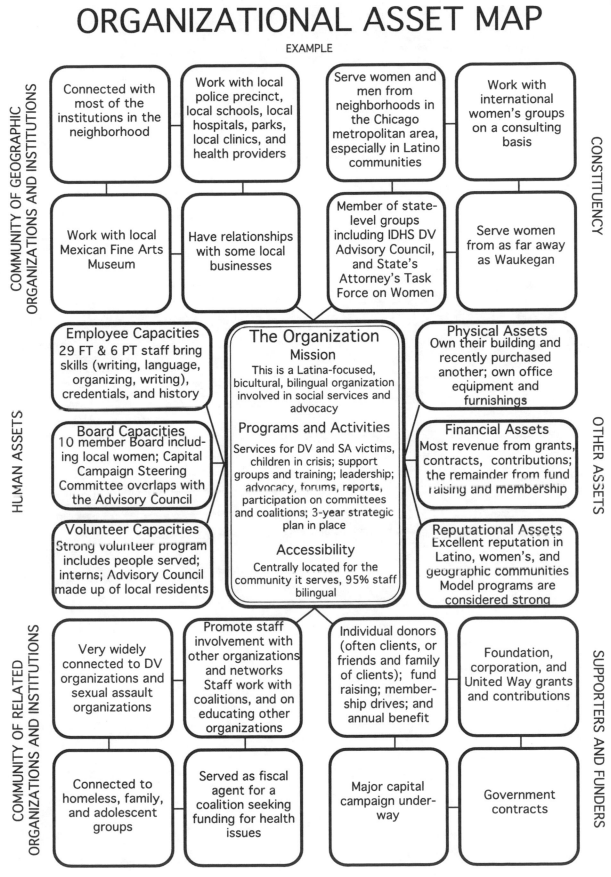

COMMUNITY OF GEOGRAPHIC ORGANIZATIONS AND INSTITUTIONS

Connected with most of the institutions in the neighborhood

Work with local police precinct, local schools, local hospitals, parks, local clinics, and health providers

Serve women and men from neighborhoods in the Chicago metropolitan area, especially in Latino communities

Work with international women's groups on a consulting basis

Work with local Mexican Fine Arts Museum

Have relationships with some local businesses

Member of state-level groups including IDHS DV Advisory Council, and State's Attorney's Task Force on Women

Serve women from as far away as Waukegan

CONSTITUENCY

HUMAN ASSETS

Employee Capacities
29 FT & 6 PT staff bring skills (writing, language, organizing, writing), credentials, and history

Board Capacities
10 member Board including local women; Capital Campaign Steering Committee overlaps with the Advisory Council

Volunteer Capacities
Strong volunteer program includes people served; interns; Advisory Council made up of local residents

The Organization
Mission
This is a Latina-focused, bicultural, bilingual organization involved in social services and advocacy

Programs and Activities
Services for DV and SA victims, children in crisis; support groups and training; leadership; advocacy, forums, reports, participation on committees and coalitions; 3-year strategic plan in place

Accessibility
Centrally located for the community it serves, 95% staff bilingual

Physical Assets
Own their building and recently purchased another; own office equipment and furnishings

Financial Assets
Most revenue from grants, contracts, contributions; the remainder from fund raising and membership

Reputational Assets
Excellent reputation in Latino, women's, and geographic communities Model programs are considered strong

OTHER ASSETS

COMMUNITY OF RELATED ORGANIZATIONS AND INSTITUTIONS

Very widely connected to DV organizations and sexual assault organizations

Promote staff involvement with other organizations and networks Staff work with coalitions, and on educating other organizations

Individual donors (often clients, or friends and family of clients); fund raising; membership drives; and annual benefit

Foundation, corporation, and United Way grants and contributions

Connected to homeless, family, and adolescent groups

Served as fiscal agent for a coalition seeking funding for health issues

Major capital campaign underway

Government contracts

SUPPORTERS AND FUNDERS

EXPLORING ORGANIZATIONAL RESILIENCY

GOALS ☞

The Goals of this Exercise are:

◆ To understand the many dimensions of the definition of organizational resiliency.

◆ To examine the organization in relationship to each component of the definition.

◆ To evaluate the degree of resiliency the organization possesses with which to meet opportunities and challenges.

LEARNING
CONCEPTS ☞

The Learning Concepts Associated with this Exercise are:

◆ *Organizational Resiliency*—Resiliency is the ability of the organization to sustain itself and carry out its mission in a situation of adversity (e.g., the loss of any key component from the organizational asset map) *and* to respond to and manage planned and unplanned change or opportunities that present themselves.

This exercise will utilize a definition of organizational resiliency developed by representatives from the diverse assembly of women's organizations who comprised the original SHOW-21 working group. This group envisioned *resiliency* as a position achieved by organizations somewhere along the pathway to the desired goal of *sustainability*. The definition reflects some degree of both stability and flexibility, both conditions seen by SHOW-21 participants as critical precursors to moving into a position of sustainability. In addition, the definition of resiliency suggests a more reactive than proactive organizational mode, that is, resiliency means an organization is able to effectively respond to the various situations it encounters. Sustainability, on the other hand, assumes more ability on the part of the organization to be proactive about using its strengths to its best advantage, rather than only responding to external pressures and opportunities.

The definition of resiliency is organized as a *statement* and a series of *supporting ideas*. While working through this exercise, remember that all organizations are different and that some components of the definition may seem more or less applicable. Pay attention to all of the supporting ideas however, because while they may seem out of reach or unrealistic in certain situations, having some level of grounding in each one contributes to an organization's resilience.

GROUP ACTIVITY

As a first step, the group should engage in a discussion that explores the meaning and characteristics of organizational resiliency. The discussion may begin independently of the definition—that is, without studying it—and provide the participants an opportunity to contribute ideas based on their own experiences. After examining the definition and its supporting ideas, the discussion may continue with an exploration of each supporting idea, its contribution to organizational resiliency, the difficulty of achieving each one, and the nature of the balance between and among them. The group should talk about which category of supporting ideas seems most critical, if any, and why certain aspects of resilience may be more important in specific situations. During the discussion, each participant should utilize a blank copy of the **Resiliency Map** to jot down thoughts about his or her own organization's level of resiliency.

ORGANIZATIONAL ACTIVITY

In additional to the group discussion of organizational resiliency, it may be useful for each organization to carry out an internal resiliency evaluation. Each member of the working group should invite others within his or her organization to participate in the process. This group may be selected from among members of the board, employees, or committee members, but should certainly include whoever is deemed an important part of the organization's development. To explore an organization's resiliency in more depth, examine each component of the definition and evaluate the organization in relationship to it, writing an assessment as a document that can be incorporated into future discussions or planning sessions. Use a blank copy of the **Resiliency Map** to illustrate the internal assessment in graphic terms.

> **Resiliency is the ability of the organization to sustain itself and carry out its mission in a situation of adversity (e.g., the loss of any key component from the organizational map) *and* to respond to and manage planned and unplanned change or opportunities that present themselves.**

A.   STRATEGIC PLANNING:

1.   Having the capacity to seize opportunity and overcome threats without compromising the mission of the organization.

2.   Conducting active strategic planning and assessment; having vision within the context of the mission.

3.   Having a board with members who have the appropriate outlook, are actively involved in decision making, and have the knowledge, time, skill, willingness, and tenaciousness to sustain the organization in times of challenge.

B.   FINANCIAL RESOURCES:

1.   Obtaining multi-dimensional funding from a variety of sources via diverse fund-raising strategies.

2.   Possessing the ability to calculate risk and the willingness to both take and refuse to take risks.

3.   Having a financial cushion sufficient to provide a margin of safety in terms of cash flow, having cash on hand to carry on through a month or more.

C.   PROGRAMMING:

1.   Carrying out the organizational mission through high-quality programming and day-to-day operations.

D.   STAFF:

1.   Nurturing employees in terms of things like (a) space, pay, and benefits, and (b) recognition, flexibility, and time.

2.   Providing targeted or more general educational opportunities for staff.

3.   Enhancing employee opportunities to utilize their skills and abilities and to identify ways they would like to contribute to the organization.

4.   Having people—specific people—involved in the organization that can provide the strength and tenacity to keep the organization going. This is particularly important when the organization is young or going through major upheavals.

E.   EVALUATION:

1.   Ongoing participatory decision making/evaluation/assessment/ leadership development among staff, board, and constituency.

F.   PUBLIC RELATIONS AND REPUTATION:

1.   Possessing a good reputation and having an appropriate level of visibility.

2. Disseminating information about and advocating for the organization; creating a strong organizational image and expressing it through the executive director, board, and staff.

3. Having strong relationships—formal and informal—and collaborations with other organizations that support and/or share the same work.

4. Having knowledge of powerful members of other sectors (e.g., political, business, civic, philanthropic, and religious), representing both allies and foes, and having relationships with these individuals where appropriate.

G. CONSTITUENCY:

1. Identifying new ways that the organization's unique access to its constituents represents a potentially powerful tool that can be utilized in organizational planning, evaluation, and promotion.

2. Maintaining strong and trusting relationships with constituencies and accepting their help in times of adversity.

TAILORED ORGANIZATIONAL ACTIVITY

Although the definition of organizational resiliency is presented in what can be considered a complete form, it is possible that other groups may want to explore and build the definition further. If this is so, it may be best to do so according to the same model shown here, that is, to identify a category and set of supporting ideas that can be framed within the notion of a resiliency map. There is no **Tailored Activity Version** of the **Resiliency Map** because this is a fairly complete activity as it stands. However, the blank copy of the **Resiliency Map** that is included may be modified if this suits the goals of other organizational sustainability working groups.

APPLICATION

Example 1:

The participating organizations in the SHOW-21 program developed the definition of resiliency as a group, and completed an organizational self-assessment independently. Working individually with the SHOW-21 consultant, each executive director explored every part of the definition in relationship to his or her own organization. Each one prepared both a text version of the resiliency map and a graphic version; both versions became part of the permanent sustainability exploration of each organization and were used extensively in strategizing new directions for growth.

RESILIENCY MAP

SHOW-21 VERSION

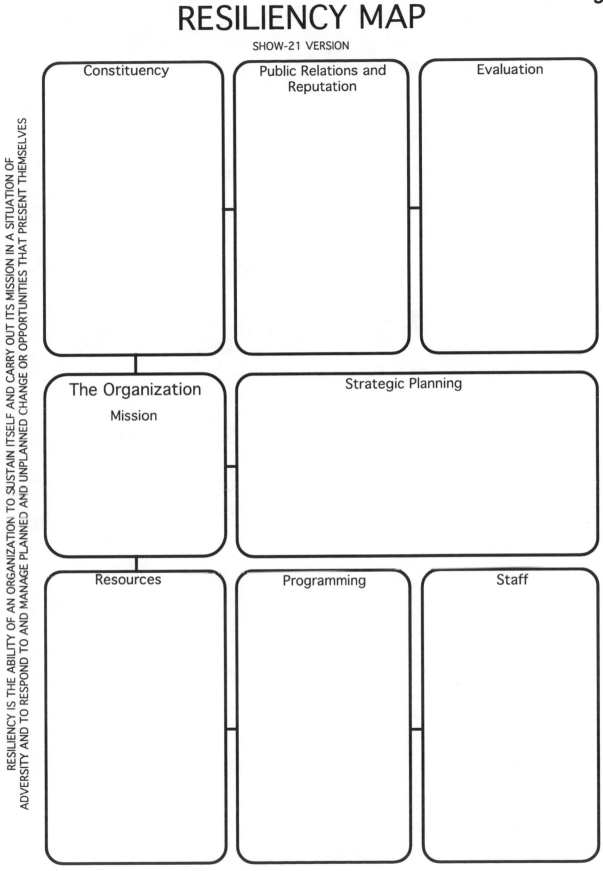

RESILIENCY IS THE ABILITY OF AN ORGANIZATION TO SUSTAIN ITSELF AND CARRY OUT ITS MISSION IN A SITUATION OF
ADVERSITY AND TO RESPOND TO AND MANAGE PLANNED AND UNPLANNED CHANGE OR OPPORTUNITIES THAT PRESENT THEMSELVES

Constituency

Public Relations and
Reputation

Evaluation

The Organization

Mission

Strategic Planning

Resources

Programming

Staff

RESILIENCY MAP

EXAMPLE

RESILIENCY IS THE ABILITY OF AN ORGANIZATION TO SUSTAIN ITSELF AND CARRY OUT ITS MISSION IN A SITUATION OF ADVERSITY AND TO RESPOND TO AND MANAGE PLANNED AND UNPLANNED CHANGE OR OPPORTUNITIES THAT PRESENT THEMSELVES

Constituency

The organization gives itself a high rating on incorporating its constituency into its work. It is exploring ways to involve young people even more than currently by giving them the opportunity to create a web site for discussion of adolescent health issues and the sharing of information.

Public Relations and Reputation

The organization gives itself a mixed rating on public relations and reputation. It has an excellent reputation in certain circles but as it deals with sensitive issues, it sometimes struggles with negative attitudes from some. Accepts that it will never please everyone, but looks for ways to expand the image of the organization.

Evaluation

The organization gives itself a high rating on evaluation. It is working towards moving beyond funder demands to doing what it takes to keep the organization running smoothly. It runs focus groups to obtain feedback from its constituents so it can understand and demonstrate that it is meeting their needs.

The Organization

Mission

The organization provides education, policy advocacy, and training on the health and well-being of adolescents and their families. In particular, in the Latino and African American communities.

Strategic Planning

The organization rates itself high in terms of strategic planning. Has recognized the value of having an up-to-date strategic plan in place. Initially developed one to satisfy a funder, but soon realized the importance of the plan for directing the organization.

Resources

The organization rates itself as adequate on financial resources. It generates funds from a variety of sources and has several sources of multi-year funding. But the organization is not completely satisfied with some of its current funding sources and considers seeking national level support.

Programming

The organization rates itself very high on programming. It provides a broad range of programs targeting adolescents and their families. It continually explores new ideas for programs that will attract young people, spark their creativity, and maintain their interest and involvement.

Staff

The organization rates itself as adequate on its ability to provide staff with what they require for sustained commitment to the organization. Developing new skills in assessing what is necessary and how to generate the necessary resources. Work environment and relationships among staff are excellent.

THINKING OUT OF THE BOX—MOBILIZING ASSETS FOR INCREASED SUSTAINABILITY

GOALS ☞

> **The Goals of this Exercise are:**
>
> ◆ To eliminate artificial constraints on thinking and get your creative juices flowing.
>
> ◆ To explore the possibilities for making better use of the existing assets within the organization to increase sustainability.
>
> ◆ To promote new ideas and non-traditional solutions that rely on organizational assets as the raw materials.

LEARNING CONCEPTS ☞

> **The Learning Concepts Associated with this Exercise are:**
>
> ◆ *Thinking Out of the Box*—getting beyond traditional or accustomed ways of thinking about organizational issues and answers; allowing the imagination to take over and explore a broad range of ideas that may never have been considered before.
>
> ◆ *Mobilizing Organizational Assets for Sustainability*—the deliberate and strategic utilization of organizational assets and capacities into every aspect of organizational activity.

Mobilizing organizational assets toward increased sustainability means taking strategic action based on the new knowledge that has been gained in this process. Just as thinking about organizational development from the assets perspective is a new way of thinking, this strategic action should emerge from the same kind of shift to thinking "outside the box" of usual day-to-day actions. As a first step, the working group should engage in some fun activities that help to promote creativity and generate ideas that come from this new way of thinking.

GROUP ACTIVITY

A good exercise to begin this process is called *You Can Market Anything*. For this exercise, break people into groups of two or three and have each group spend 20 minutes developing a marketing plan for a new product. The objective of this exercise is to get the group to start thinking "out of the box," that is, to eliminate any artificial barriers to a positive attitude. The product can be anything, but should be something beyond the realm of usual thinking, for example, men's pantyhose. The participants should be sure to use their own personal capacities in the marketing plan. Each group should then share its plan with the other participants. The results are often silly, but tend to be very imaginative.

As a second step, the working group can reflect on the lessons they have learned together in the process of producing individual organizational asset maps and using the other tools in the SHOW-21 Tool Box. They should then combine the creativity that just surfaced through the Thinking Out of the Box exercise with the reflections and apply them to a hypothetical organizational challenge. Throughout this part of the exercise, the working group should pay attention to applying both lessons learned and creative thinking about assets to the situation defined for them. The discussion should produce a strategic action plan that mobilizes as many organizational assets as possible.

ORGANIZATIONAL ACTIVITY

In additional to the group discussion of mobilizing organizational assets, it is useful for each organization to explore internal opportunities for asset mobilization. Mobilizing assets may take the form of adding something entirely new or building new relevance into a component that already exists. This exercise may be carried as an organizational activity, and the participants may be selected from among members of the board, employees, or whatever part of the organization seems most appropriate. To experiment with possible mobilizing strategies, use the following questions as a guide. The goal is to identify as many opportunities for a new kind of action as possible. A written document can be prepared in responding to the questions and can be used for strategic planning purposes. Use a blank copy of the **Asset Mobilizing Map** to illustrate strategies developed in graphic terms.

A.   THE ORGANIZATION ITSELF:

1.   What new programs and/or activities might the organization develop?

2. How could you make the organization more accessible (e.g., services to a new set of constituents; promotion of your location)?

B. THE ORGANIZATION'S HUMAN ASSETS AND CAPACITIES:

1. In what ways could you identify and mobilize currently untapped employee capacities (e.g., develop a program around a particular skill)?

2. In what ways could you identify and mobilize currently untapped board member capacities (e.g., tap into board member corporate connections)?

3. In what ways could you identify and mobilize currently untapped volunteer capacities (e.g., offer imaginative involvement opportunities based on what volunteers would like to contribute)?

C. THE PHYSICAL/FINANCIAL/REPUTATIONAL ASSETS:

1. How could you get more from your physical assets, or positively transform this component of your asset map (e.g., share space or equipment with another organization; rent some of your space)?

2. How could you get more from your financial assets, or positively transform this component of your asset map (e.g., develop new funding streams; develop a for-profit activity)?

3. How could you get more from your reputational assets, or positively transform this component of your asset map (e.g., marketing efforts)?

D. THE CONSTITUENCY:

1. In what ways could you mobilize the capacities of the individuals you currently serve on behalf of the organization (e.g., as spokespersons or in fund-raising efforts)?

2. In what ways could you mobilize the capacities of individuals you have served in the past on behalf of the organization (e.g., as spokespersons or employees)?

E. COMMUNITY OF RELATED ORGANIZATIONS AND INSTITUTIONS:

1. In what ways could you mobilize the assets and capacities of the other organizations and institutions with whom you have relationships on behalf of the organization (e.g., developing joint programming; sharing employee expertise)?

F. THE COMMUNITY OF LOCATION:

1. In what ways could you mobilize the assets and capacities of the other organizations and institutions in your geographic area on behalf of the organization (e.g., buying materials from local suppliers; hiring locally)?

G. THE SUPPORTERS AND FUNDERS:

1. In what ways could you mobilize the assets and capacities of your supporters and funders on behalf of the organization (e.g., inviting members to increase their involvement; asking funders to support innovative capacity-building activities)?

TAILORED ORGANIZATIONAL ACTIVITY

The asset-mobilizing exploration is undoubtedly best accomplished by tailoring the process to each specific organization. Each organization is encouraged to make whatever modifications seem appropriate in order to make the most of the asset-mobilizing process. A completely blank **Asset Mobilizing Map (Tailored Activity Version)** suitable for modifying is provided for a more individualized approach to the activity. With this version of the map, each organization can select the categories that best describe its own organizational activities and community milieus and enter them as headings on the blank map. The guiding questions can then be adjusted to reflect the new headings. Tailored maps also represent a valuable learning tool and can be shared with the larger working group.

APPLICATION

Example 1:

Each organization in the SHOW-21 program worked with the **Asset Mobilizing Map** to develop a set of asset-mobilizing strategies specific to its own organization's needs. For some, this meant revisiting previously developed plans and modifying them to incorporate new perspectives on the assets that might be available to impact the activity but which had not been thought of earlier. For others, this meant developing entirely new strategies based on assets newly identified.

Example 2:

A nonprofit organization involved in the development of both a health professionals curriculum and community-based definitions of health used the **Asset Mobilizing Map** to explore directions its efforts could take in terms of providing medical and nursing students opportunities for studying health within a community setting. By identifying the full range of human assets—physicians, nurses, hospital staff, students, and community members—that could be part of their strategies, and exploring different ways to mobilize those assets, the organization created a new strategic plan, its health professionals curriculum has been widely accepted in medical and nursing schools, and the organization has developed a new funding stream based on its publications.

ASSET MOBILIZING MAP

SHOW-21 VERSION

61

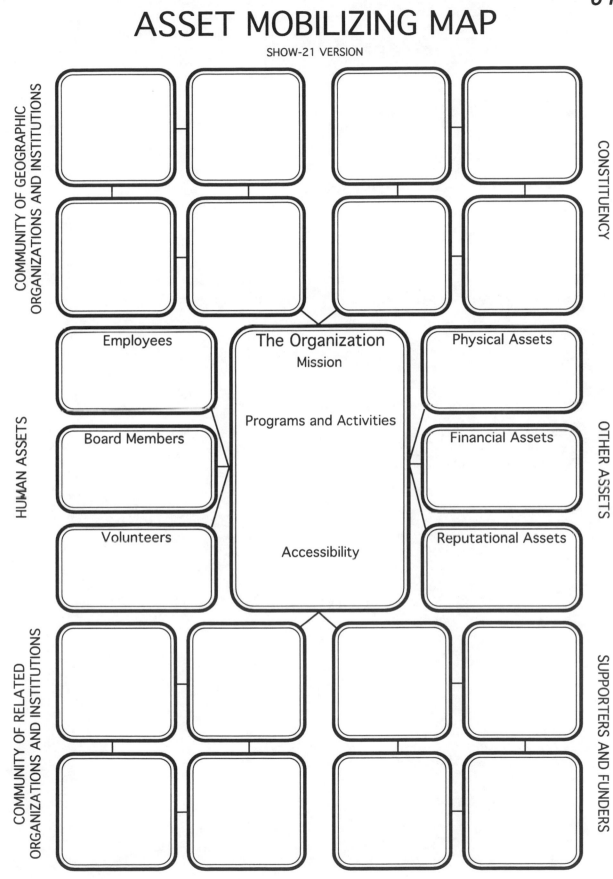

COMMUNITY OF GEOGRAPHIC ORGANIZATIONS AND INSTITUTIONS

CONSTITUENCY

HUMAN ASSETS

Employees

Board Members

Volunteers

The Organization

Mission

Programs and Activities

Accessibility

Physical Assets

Financial Assets

Reputational Assets

OTHER ASSETS

COMMUNITY OF RELATED ORGANIZATIONS AND INSTITUTIONS

SUPPORTERS AND FUNDERS

ASSET MOBILIZING MAP

TAILORED ACTIVITY VERSION

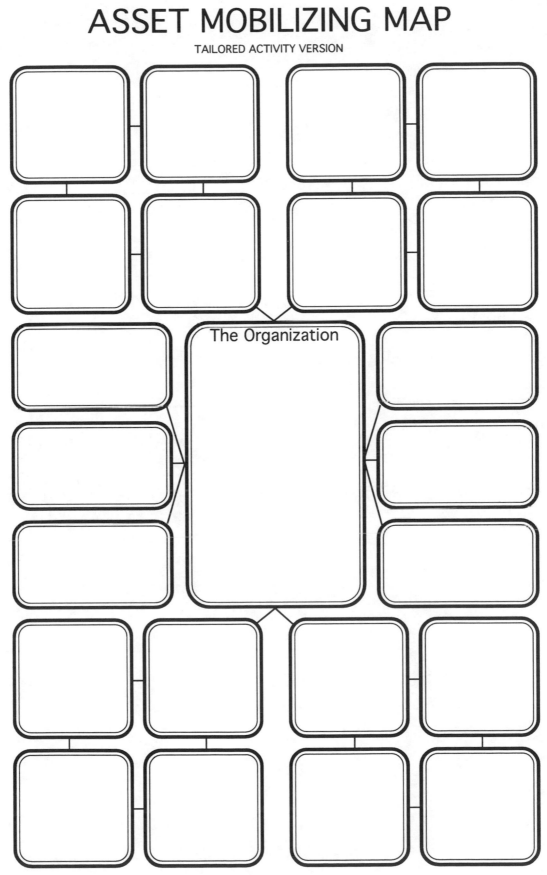

The Organization

ASSET MOBILIZING MAP

EXAMPLE

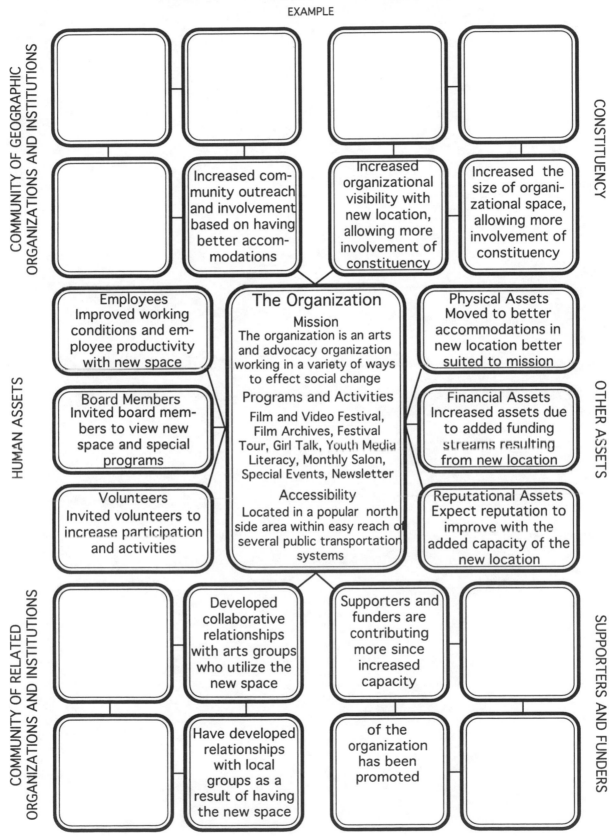

COMMUNITY OF GEOGRAPHIC ORGANIZATIONS AND INSTITUTIONS

CONSTITUENCY

Increased community outreach and involvement based on having better accommodations

Increased organizational visibility with new location, allowing more involvement of constituency

Increased the size of organizational space, allowing more involvement of constituency

HUMAN ASSETS

Employees Improved working conditions and employee productivity with new space

Board Members Invited board members to view new space and special programs

Volunteers Invited volunteers to increase participation and activities

The Organization

Mission
The organization is an arts and advocacy organization working in a variety of ways to effect social change

Programs and Activities
Film and Video Festival, Film Archives, Festival Tour, Girl Talk, Youth Media Literacy, Monthly Salon, Special Events, Newsletter

Accessibility
Located in a popular north side area within easy reach of several public transportation systems

OTHER ASSETS

Physical Assets Moved to better accommodations in new location better suited to mission

Financial Assets Increased assets due to added funding streams resulting from new location

Reputational Assets Expect reputation to improve with the added capacity of the new location

COMMUNITY OF RELATED ORGANIZATIONS AND INSTITUTIONS

SUPPORTERS AND FUNDERS

Developed collaborative relationships with arts groups who utilize the new space

Supporters and funders are contributing more since increased capacity

Have developed relationships with local groups as a result of having the new space

of the organization has been promoted

EXPLORING ORGANIZATIONAL SUSTAINABILITY

GOALS ☞

> **The Goals of this Exercise are:**
>
> ◆ To understand the many dimensions of the definition of organizational sustainability.
>
> ◆ To examine the organization in relationship to each component of the definition.
>
> ◆ To evaluate the level of sustainability the organization has achieved.
>
> ◆ To explore possible areas for organizational development in order to increase sustainability.

LEARNING CONCEPTS ☞

> **The Learning Concepts Associated with this Exercise are:**
>
> ◆ *Organizational Sustainability*—the capacity of an organization to effectively mobilize its assets toward generating the ongoing resources necessary to maintain the mission and carry out high-quality work in an environment that reinforces the well-being and creativity of the individuals involved.

This exercise utilizes a definition of organizational sustainability that was developed by representatives from a diverse assembly of women's organizations who comprised the original SHOW-21 working group. This group envisioned *sustainability* as a position achieved by organizations that have generally been able to identify and effectively mobilize their assets toward generating the ongoing resources necessary to maintain the mission and carry out high-quality work. The definition is organized as a *statement* and a series of *supporting ideas*. As the group works through this exercise, remember that all organizations are different and that some components of the definition may seem more or less applicable. Pay attention to all of the supporting ideas, however, because while they may seem out of reach or unrealistic in certain situations, having a grounding in each one contributes to an organization's sustainability.

GROUP ACTIVITY

As a first step, the group should engage in a discussion that explores the meaning and characteristics of organizational sustainability. This discussion may begin without first studying the definition presented here, allowing participants to contribute ideas based on their own experiences. Then, examine the definition, including its statement and supporting ideas. The discussion may then continue by exploring each supporting idea, its contribution to organizational sustainability, the difficulty of achieving each one, and the nature of the balance between and among them. The group should address which category of supporting ideas seems most critical, if any, and why certain aspects of sustainability may be more important in specific situations. During the discussion, all participants should utilize a blank copy of the **Sustainability Map** to jot down thoughts about their own organization's level of sustainability.

ORGANIZATIONAL ACTIVITY

In additional to the group discussion of organizational sustainability, it is useful for each organization to carry out an internal sustainability evaluation. This exercise should be carried as an organizational activity, and the participants may be selected from among members of the board, employees, or whatever part of the organization seems appropriate. To explore an organization's sustainability in more depth, examine each component of the definition and evaluate the organization in relationship to it, writing the assessment as a document that can be incorporated into future discussions or planning sessions. Use a blank copy of the **Sustainability Map** to illustrate the assessment in graphic terms.

Sustainability is the capacity of an organization to effectively mobilize its assets toward generating the ongoing resources necessary to maintain the mission and carry out high-quality work in an environment that reinforces the well-being and creativity of the individuals involved.

Note: This definition was developed by organizations that consider themselves progressive, feminist, agents for social change. The first three specific characteristics of sustainability therefore reflect a set of assumptions that can be viewed as guiding principles for organizations sharing this philosophy.

A. GUIDING PRINCIPLES:

1. Accomplishing goals in an effective way; being a dynamic, exciting organization that responds to a real-world, progressive, women's agenda.

2. Being a change agent in addition to being capable of change; having the willingness and ability to push hard on tough issues and be a voice for serious social reform.

3. Incorporating ethics and values into the organization at every level; demanding a higher level of commitment to principles as a fundamental component of best practices for women's organizations.

B. ORGANIZATIONAL DEVELOPMENT:

1. Achieving depth and solidity in each of the components of resiliency.

2. Escaping from the sense of immediacy; day-to-day operations move along smoothly in an overall situation of reduced struggle.

3. Developing enough organizational equilibrium to step back and engage in deep thinking. Deep thinking is the opposite of emergency thinking, it requires time and space in which to let go of day-to-day issues and focus on the long view.

4. Possessing an awareness of what the appropriate size and range of activities is for the organization (i.e., knowing when to grow and when to stop growing, knowing that an effective organization must sometimes limit the scope of what it does). Gaining confidence that the organization can be sustained in the absence of continual growth.

5. Integrating the voices of the constituency and making them central to as many aspects of organizational planning and strategizing as possible.

C. ORGANIZATIONAL LIFE COURSE:

1. Gaining sufficient experience with the long-term organizational life course so that a map of the direction the organization is heading—with some degree of flexibility built in—can be projected.

2. Understanding the annual cycle of the organization and how specific cycles are both distinct and dependent on those preceding and following them. Managing the organizational time line of activities and funding streams effectively, and providing appropriate stewardship of resources in relationship to annual cycles.

3. Maintaining the relevance of the organizational mission; having the ability/expertise/insight to reframe or recast the organization and its

programs according to the changing realities and dynamics of the larger world.

4. Achieving a condition of solidity that can withstand the flux of major change; recognizing options at major organizational decision points and choosing the most appropriate from within a range of options including:

   a. Carrying on with what the organization is currently doing;

   b. Transforming the organization to meet either the demands of a new external situation or the strengths and abilities of the existing organization;

   c. Merging the organization with another related or different organization;

   d. Dissolving the organization.

TAILORED ORGANIZATIONAL ACTIVITY

Although the definition of organizational sustainability is presented in a fairly complete form, it is possible that other groups may want to explore and build the definition further. If this is so, do so according to the same model used here, that is, identify a category and set of supporting ideas that can be framed within the notion of a sustainability map. A **Tailored Activity Version** of the **Sustainability Map** is not included here because this is a fairly complete activity as it stands. However, the blank copy of the **Sustainability Map** that is included may be modified if this suits the goals of the organizational sustainability working group.

APPLICATION

Example 1:

The SHOW-21 participants worked together to develop the definition of sustainability based on their own experiences and their own visions for how they wanted their organizations to function. Each organization used the sustainability map to examine their own organization individually and to develop both a text and a graphic version of the work. Many of the original SHOW-21 organizations have used their sustainability maps as a visioning tool because it enables them to see the places within their organizations where capacity building is required.

Example 2:

A group of nonprofit organizations working together in a group developed their own definition for sustainability and then compared it to the SHOW-21 version. Their initial discussion provoked so much thought and so many ideas that they decided to move forward with their own version of the definition. When they compared the definition to the one developed in SHOW-21, they discovered the same categories of characteristics and very similar details among the supporting ideas. Like the SHOW-21 definition, these organizations envisioned sustainability as a more proactive quality than resiliency.

SUSTAINABILITY MAP

SHOW-21 VERSION

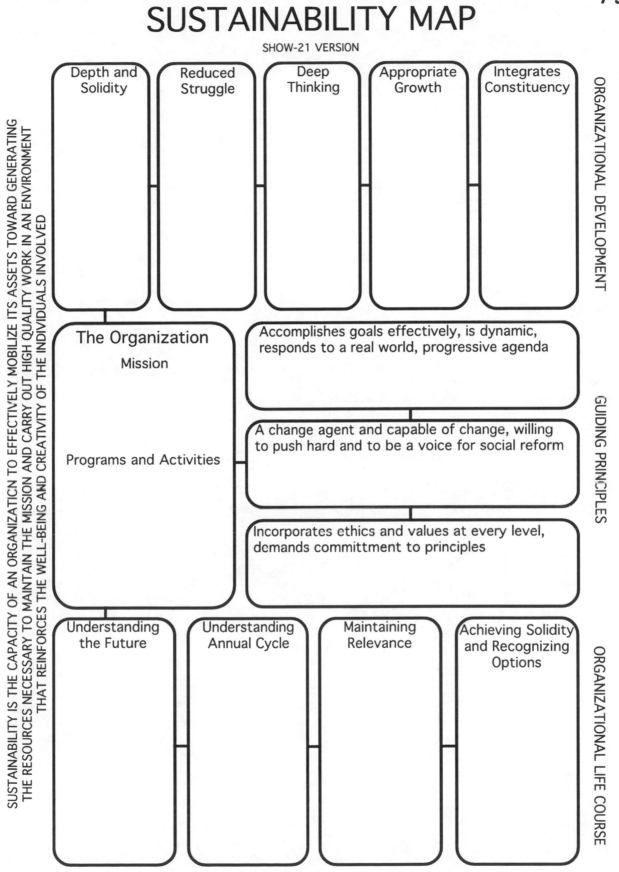

SUSTAINABILITY IS THE CAPACITY OF AN ORGANIZATION TO EFFECTIVELY MOBILIZE ITS ASSETS TOWARD GENERATING THE RESOURCES NECESSARY TO MAINTAIN THE MISSION AND CARRY OUT HIGH QUALITY WORK IN AN ENVIRONMENT THAT REINFORCES THE WELL-BEING AND CREATIVITY OF THE INDIVIDUALS INVOLVED

ORGANIZATIONAL DEVELOPMENT

| Depth and Solidity | Reduced Struggle | Deep Thinking | Appropriate Growth | Integrates Constituency |

The Organization

Mission

Programs and Activities

Accomplishes goals effectively, is dynamic, responds to a real world, progressive agenda

A change agent and capable of change, willing to push hard and to be a voice for social reform

Incorporates ethics and values at every level, demands committment to principles

GUIDING PRINCIPLES

| Understanding the Future | Understanding Annual Cycle | Maintaining Relevance | Achieving Solidity and Recognizing Options |

ORGANIZATIONAL LIFE COURSE

SUSTAINABILITY MAP

EXAMPLE

ORGANIZATIONAL DEVELOPMENT

Depth and Solidity

Executive director, staff and board are well-versed and comfortable with what the organization is and are able to articulate the mission effectively

Reduced Struggle

Salaries are at an appropriate level; benefits have been included in the compensation package; staff work regular hours for the most part

Deep Thinking

The executive director has been able to rely on staff for everyday organizational activities so that she can take the time to engage in creative thinking about organizational development

Appropriate Growth

The organization decided against one opportunity for growth that was not in line with the mission, but took advantage of an opportunity to grow a new small program

Integrates Constituency

Executive director, staff, and board are working on several plans for constituent involvement in promoting the work of the organization

The Organization

Mission
To provide health education to minority youth in an environment of acceptance and tolerance

Programs and Activities

Health education for young people including reproductive health; peer mentoring programs; youth clinic

GUIDING PRINCIPLES

Accomplishes goals effectively, is dynamic, responds to a real world, progressive agenda
The organization operates on the principle that every individual is entitled to knowledge about health issues as well as health care

A change agent and capable of change, willing to push hard and to be a voice for social reform
The organization works hard to promote health education within the schools and other local institutions in order to reach more young people

Incorporates ethics and values at every level, demands committment to principles
The organization is deeply committed to the principle of providing appropriate health education to youth who might otherwise have no access to it

ORGANIZATIONAL LIFE COURSE

Understanding the Future

Executive director, staff, and board have been involved in developing a strategic plan which projects the organization's growth and activities for the next five years; each person understands the organization from the broader perspective

Understanding Annual Cycle

Executive director has worked with the board and staff to educate them about typical changes that occur throughout the year and over the course of funding cycles; board and staff are now better prepared for leaner periods and times of stress

Maintaining Relevance

The organization recognizes that one of its programs may have outlived its relevance and is considering developing a new program with more relevance in the lives of young people

Achieving Solidity and Recognizing Options

Currently, the organization is comfortably situated both physically and financially and is unconcerned about the immediate future; feels able to take advantage of opportunities that become available

MAPPING EMPLOYEE ASSETS

GOALS ☞

> **The Goals of this Exercise are:**
>
> ♦ To think about each individual employee in a multi-dimensional way and develop a more complete view of who the employee really is and what he or she contributes to the overall organizational asset map.
>
> ♦ To identify what each employee would most like to be doing within the organization and what responsibilities would make the most of their capacities.
>
> ♦ To identify ways to connect each employee's interests and abilities with the most appropriate responsibilities within the organization.
>
> ♦ To expand the avenues for contribution to the organization based on what each employee brings to the table.
>
> ♦ To identify opportunities for employee development in terms of training, education, and leadership.

LEARNING
CONCEPTS ☞

> **The Learning Concepts Associated with this Exercise are:**
>
> ♦ *Employee Assets*—the total of all of the capacities brought to the organization by each employee, plus their connections, relationships, and personal potential represent the full measure of employee assets.
>
> ♦ *Employee Capacities*—the specific skills, abilities, interests, and experiences that individual employees bring to their work with the organization.

For this exercise, try to think more deeply about who each employee really is in terms of the many capacities each brings to work with the organization and how each one represents a part of the organization's employee assets. Employees are often thought of primarily in terms of the specific job they do, and organizations sometimes fail to explore more deeply what contributions each one might make if more were known about them. If an organization is successful in really knowing its employees, it is more able to develop the kinds of opportunities for involvement that will fully utilize and reward each individual. This exercise provides the opportunity to examine employee capacities and how they fit into what is happening at the organization, and also to explore how their capacities might be better utilized based on their own interests and potential.

GROUP ACTIVITY

For the group activity, each participant should use a blank copy of the **Employee Asset Map (SHOW-21 Version)** included at the end of this section. Group members should spend about 20 minutes thinking independently and filling in the boxes on the worksheet. At the end of this period, all participants should share something about the specific employee assets they were able to identify. A discussion can then occur among the group about how much participants actually know about their employees and what they included on their asset map. The discussion should spark new ideas for everyone about what kinds of things may be viewed as employee assets.

ORGANIZATIONAL ACTIVITY

The completion of the final employee map should be accomplished as an internal activity within each organization. Each individual should invite others within the organization to assist in the process. This activity may be carried out as an organizational activity, in which case the group may be selected from among members of the board, committee members, or others, or it may be viewed as an activity most suitable for employees to carry out among themselves. The goal is to generate a visual and text-based map of the organization's employee assets and capacities. The following questions may be used as a guide for exploring the organization's employee assets in an in-depth manner. The written answers to the questions form the text-based asset map; when transferred to the appropriate boxes of the **Employee Asset Map (SHOW-21 version)**, a visual version is produced. Once each organization has completed a visual and text version of the map, the working group can come together again to learn about how other participating organizations see their employees as assets and how they might mobilize these employee assets more fully.

A. CONTRIBUTIONS AND INTERESTS WITHIN THE ORGANIZATION:

1. What skills—general and specific—does the employee possess? Be sure to explore those skills that may be beyond the scope of the work the employee currently does for the organization.

2. What special qualifications does the employee possess? Are they currently using these qualifications in their work for the organization?

3. How much does the employee work? Would the employee prefer to work more or less than he or she currently does?

4. Is the employee happiest when working with others or working independently? Is this preference accommodated within the employee's job description?

5. What interests—general and specific—does the employee possess? Be sure to explore those interests that may be beyond the scope of the work the employee currently does for the organization.

6. In which of the organization's programs or activities is the employee most interested? Is this interest accommodated in the employee's job description?

7. What are the employee's actual responsibilities? Might they be changed in order to allow the organization to tap into more of the employee's capacities?

B. CONNECTIONS OUTSIDE THE ORGANIZATION:

1. What business and corporate connections does the employee possess?

2. What kinds of connections does the employee possess with other professionals?

3. What connections does the employee have with government entities?

4. What connections does the employee have with related organizations or other nonprofit organizations?

5. What assets does the employee possess in terms of family connections, activities and relationships in his or her personal life, religious commitments?

6. What other assets does the employee possess in terms of connections outside the organization?

7. Are these assets in the form of connections outside the organization being utilized to the fullest in terms of the contribution the employee makes to the organization?

TAILORED ORGANIZATIONAL ACTIVITY

It is possible that the completion of the final employee asset map may be best accomplished by tailoring the process to each specific organization. Each organization is encouraged to make whatever modifications seem appropriate in order to make the most of the asset-mapping process. A completely blank **Employee Asset Map (Tailored Activity Version)** suitable for modifying is provided for a more individualized approach to the activity. With this version of the map, each organization can select the categories that best describe its own organizational and community milieus and enter them as headings on the blank map. The guiding questions can then be adjusted to reflect the new headings. Tailored maps also represent a valuable learning tool and can be shared with the larger working group.

APPLICATION

Example 1:

One organization asked its employees to participate in an asset-mapping project at a staff retreat, and they discovered all sorts of assets among employees of which no one had been aware. One employee revealed a number of interests that would be relevant to her making a shift from one position to another, a change she was hoping to make but hesitant to ask about. She made the change and she enjoys and is growing in her new position, as well as putting her personal assets and capacities to better use.

Example 2:

Another organization discovered that one of its employees was the daughter of a woman directing a small business incubator nearby. Through this connection the organization was able to hire quality, inexpensive assistance for accounting purposes and to find a technical advisor for its computer systems. The organization benefited and the employee felt good about helping to facilitate the connection.

EMPLOYEE ASSET MAP

SHOW-21 VERSION

CONNECTIONS OUTSIDE THE ORGANIZATION

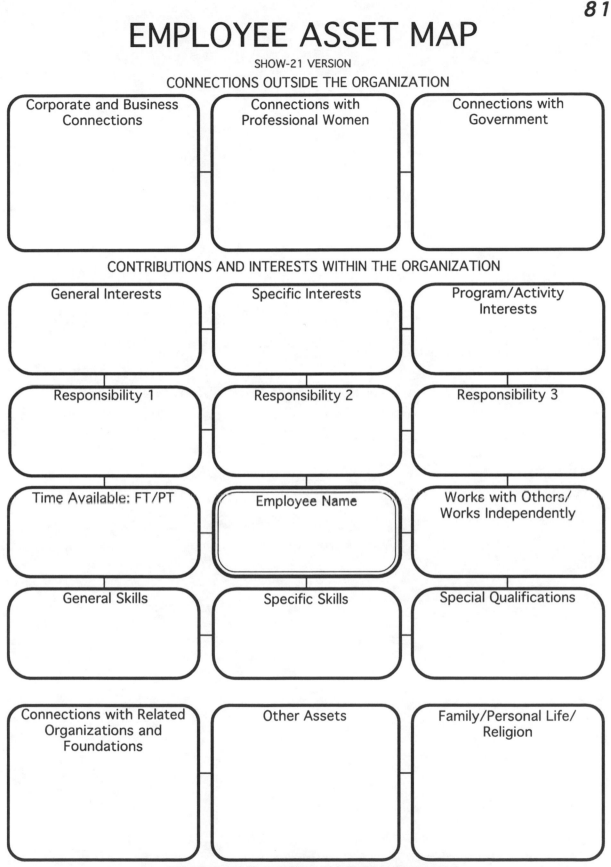

Corporate and Business Connections	Connections with Professional Women	Connections with Government

CONTRIBUTIONS AND INTERESTS WITHIN THE ORGANIZATION

General Interests	Specific Interests	Program/Activity Interests

Responsibility 1	Responsibility 2	Responsibility 3

Time Available: FT/PT	Employee Name	Works with Others/ Works Independently

General Skills	Specific Skills	Special Qualifications

Connections with Related Organizations and Foundations	Other Assets	Family/Personal Life/ Religion

CONNECTIONS OUTSIDE THE ORGANIZATION

EMPLOYEE ASSET MAP

TAILORED ACTIVITY VERSION

CONNECTIONS OUTSIDE THE ORGANIZATION

CONTRIBUTIONS AND INTERESTS WITHIN THE ORGANIZATION

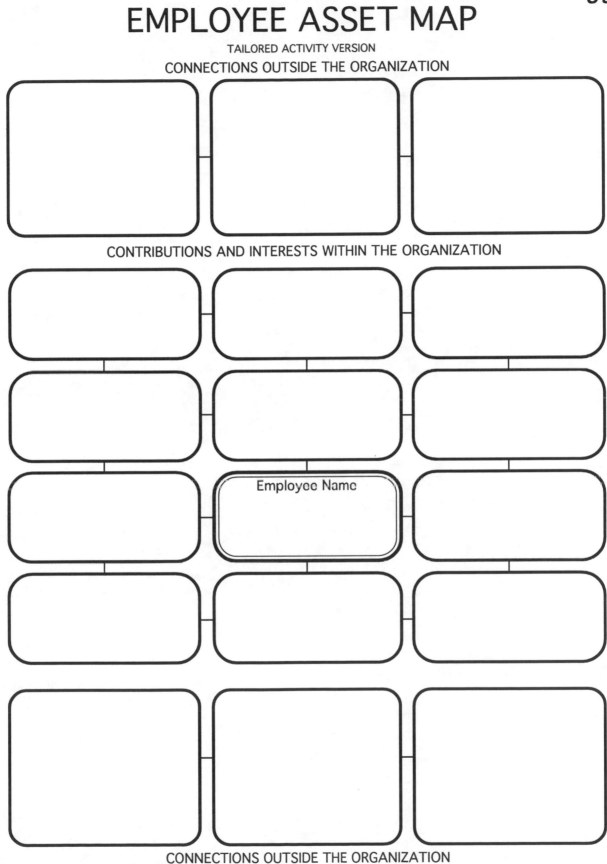

Employee Name

CONNECTIONS OUTSIDE THE ORGANIZATION

© 2000 Chicago Foundation for Women

EMPLOYEE ASSET MAP

EXAMPLE

CONNECTIONS OUTSIDE THE ORGANIZATION

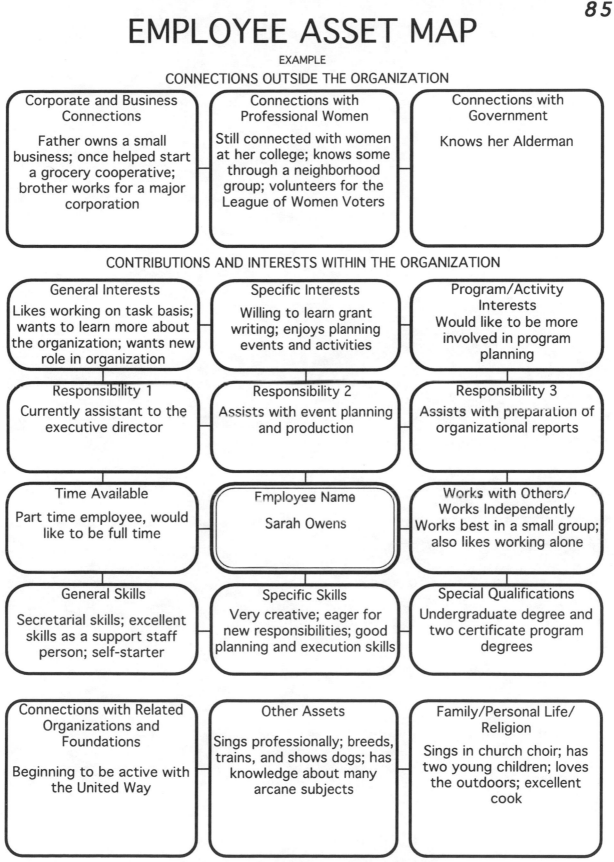

Corporate and Business Connections

Father owns a small business; once helped start a grocery cooperative; brother works for a major corporation

Connections with Professional Women

Still connected with women at her college; knows some through a neighborhood group; volunteers for the League of Women Voters

Connections with Government

Knows her Alderman

CONTRIBUTIONS AND INTERESTS WITHIN THE ORGANIZATION

General Interests
Likes working on task basis; wants to learn more about the organization; wants new role in organization

Specific Interests
Willing to learn grant writing; enjoys planning events and activities

Program/Activity Interests
Would like to be more involved in program planning

Responsibility 1
Currently assistant to the executive director

Responsibility 2
Assists with event planning and production

Responsibility 3
Assists with preparation of organizational reports

Time Available
Part time employee, would like to be full time

Employee Name
Sarah Owens

Works with Others/ Works Independently
Works best in a small group; also likes working alone

General Skills
Secretarial skills; excellent skills as a support staff person; self-starter

Specific Skills
Very creative; eager for new responsibilities; good planning and execution skills

Special Qualifications
Undergraduate degree and two certificate program degrees

Connections with Related Organizations and Foundations

Beginning to be active with the United Way

Other Assets

Sings professionally; breeds, trains, and shows dogs; has knowledge about many arcane subjects

Family/Personal Life/ Religion

Sings in church choir; has two young children; loves the outdoors; excellent cook

CONNECTIONS OUTSIDE THE ORGANIZATION

MAPPING BOARD MEMBER ASSETS

GOALS ☞

> **The Goals of this Exercise are:**
>
> ♦ To think about each individual in a multi-dimensional way and develop a more complete view of who the board member really is and what assets he or she represents.
>
> ♦ To identify what the board member would most like to be doing for the organization and what responsibilities would make the most of his or her assets.
>
> ♦ To connect the board member's interests and abilities with the most appropriate contribution within the organization.
>
> ♦ To expand the avenues for contribution to the organization based on what each board member brings to the table.
>
> ♦ To identify opportunities for board member development in terms of training, education, and leadership.

LEARNING
CONCEPTS ☞

> **The Learning Concepts Associated with this Exercise are:**
>
> ♦ *Board Member Assets*—the total of all of the capacities brought to the organization by individual board members, plus their connections, relationships, and personal potential represent the full measure of board member assets.
>
> ♦ *Board Member Capacities*—the specific skills, abilities, interests, and experiences that individual board members bring to their work with the organization.

For this exercise, try to think more deeply about who each board member really is in terms of the many capacities each one brings to his or her work with the organization and how each one represents a part of the organization's board member assets. Board members are sometimes thought of primarily in terms of the specific assignment they undertake—often related to raising money—and organizations sometimes fail to explore more deeply what contributions they might make if more were known about them. An organization that is successful in really knowing its board members is more able to develop the kinds of opportunities for involvement that will fully utilize and reward each individual. This exercise provides the opportunity to examine board member capacities and how they fit into what is happening at the organization, and also to explore how their capacities might be better utilized based on their own interests and potential.

GROUP ACTIVITY

For the group activity, each participant should use a blank copy of the **Board Member Asset Map (SHOW-21 Version)** included at the end of this section. Group members should spend about 20 minutes thinking independently and filling in the boxes on the worksheet. At the end of this period, participants should share with the group something about the specific board member assets they were able to identify. A discussion can then occur among the group about how much participants actually know about their board members and what they included on their asset map. The discussion should spark new ideas for everyone about what kinds of things may be viewed as board member assets.

ORGANIZATIONAL ACTIVITY

The completion of the final board member asset map should be accomplished as an internal activity within each organization. This activity may be carried out as an organizational activity, in which case the group may be selected from whatever parts of the organization seem appropriate, or it may be viewed as an activity most suitable for board members to carry out among themselves. The goal is to generate a visual and text-based map of the organization's board member assets and capacities. The following questions may be used as a guide for exploring the organization's board member assets in an in-depth manner. The written answers to the questions form the text-based asset map; when transferred to the appropriate boxes of the **Board Member Asset Map (SHOW-21 version)**, a visual version is produced. Once each organization has completed a visual and text version of the map, the working group can come together again to learn about how other participating organizations see their board members as assets and how they might mobilize these assets more fully.

A. CONTRIBUTIONS AND INTERESTS WITHIN THE ORGANIZATION:

1. What specific activities is the board member committed to working on throughout the year?

2. What roles and responsibilities does the board member undertake for each of these activities?

3. Do these activities, roles, and responsibilities make the most of the skills and interests of the board member, and allow her to make the most meaningful contribution possible?

4. Would the board member like to be undertaking more on behalf of the organization?

5. Have appropriate avenues for increased involvement been offered or discussed?

B. CONNECTIONS OUTSIDE THE ORGANIZATION:

1. What business and corporate connections does the board member possess?

2. What kinds of connections does the board member possess with other professionals?

3. What connections does the board member have with government entities?

4. What connections does the board member have with related organizations or other nonprofit organizations?

5. What connections does the board member have with other foundations?

6. What assets does the board member possess in terms of family connections, activities and relationships in his or her personal life, religious commitments?

7. What other assets does the board member possess in terms of connections outside the organization?

8. Are these assets in the form of connections outside the organization being utilized to the fullest in terms of the contribution the board member makes to the organization?

TAILORED ORGANIZATIONAL ACTIVITY

It is possible that the completion of the final board member asset map may be best accomplished by tailoring the process to each specific organization. Each organization is encouraged to make whatever modifications seem appropriate in order to make the most of the asset-mapping process. A completely blank **Board Member Asset Map (Tailored Activity Version)** suitable for modifying is provided for a more individualized approach to the activity. With this version of the map, each organization can select the categories that best describe its own organizational activities and milieus and enter them as headings on the blank map. The guiding questions can then be adjusted to reflect the new headings. Tailored maps also represent a valuable learning tool and can be shared with the larger working group.

APPLICATION

Example 1:

The Chicago Foundation for Women used the Board Member Asset Mapping tool at a board retreat to encourage serious thinking by members about how they most wanted to relate to and contribute to the organization. Before the retreat, one member had considered leaving the board because she felt dissatisfied with the contribution she was making and the work she was being asked to do. After going through the mapping process, she realized that rather than investing time in a number of smaller projects throughout the year, her most meaningful contribution would be to help plan and leverage an appropriate site for the Annual Luncheon. By participating actively in one large and important project, she was able to reduce her frustration, feel that her contribution was meaningful, and generate new enthusiasm for her board membership. By accommodating her needs, the foundation retained a desirable board member and gained her renewed commitment to the organization.

Example 2:

Another organization used the Board Member Asset Mapping tool at a board meeting to reassign responsibilities for the coming year. By going through the mapping process, more than half of the board members realized that they possessed some kind of asset that was being underutilized in their work with the organization. Each one was able to identify an activity that would provide an opportunity to contribute this asset to the organization. At the end of the meeting, many roles and responsibilities had been adjusted, and members felt excited about taking on tasks that interested them.

BOARD MEMBER ASSET MAP

SHOW-21 VERSION

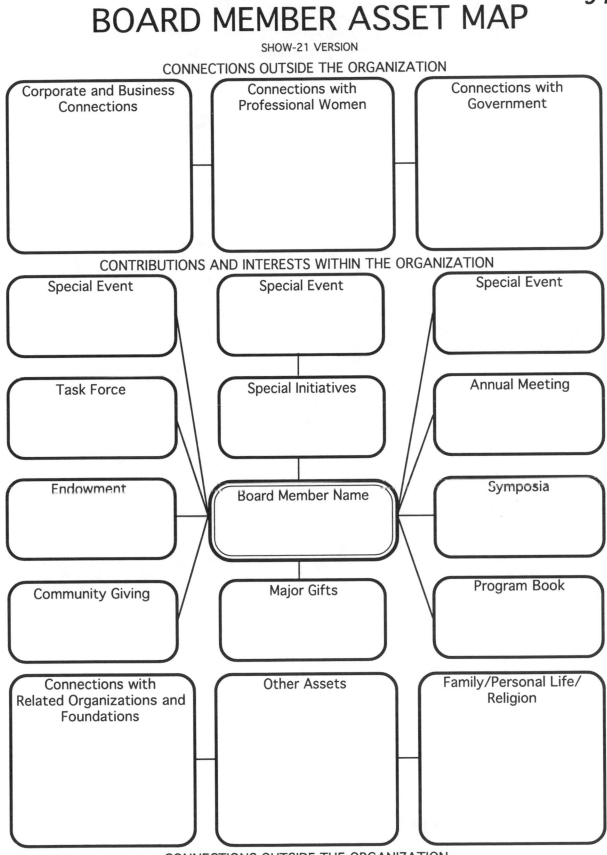

CONNECTIONS OUTSIDE THE ORGANIZATION

| Corporate and Business Connections | Connections with Professional Women | Connections with Government |

CONTRIBUTIONS AND INTERESTS WITHIN THE ORGANIZATION

Special Event | Special Event | Special Event

Task Force | Special Initiatives | Annual Meeting

Endowment | Board Member Name | Symposia

Community Giving | Major Gifts | Program Book

| Connections with Related Organizations and Foundations | Other Assets | Family/Personal Life/Religion |

CONNECTIONS OUTSIDE THE ORGANIZATION

BOARD MEMBER ASSET MAP

TAILORED ACTIVITY VERSION

CONNECTIONS OUTSIDE THE ORGANIZATION

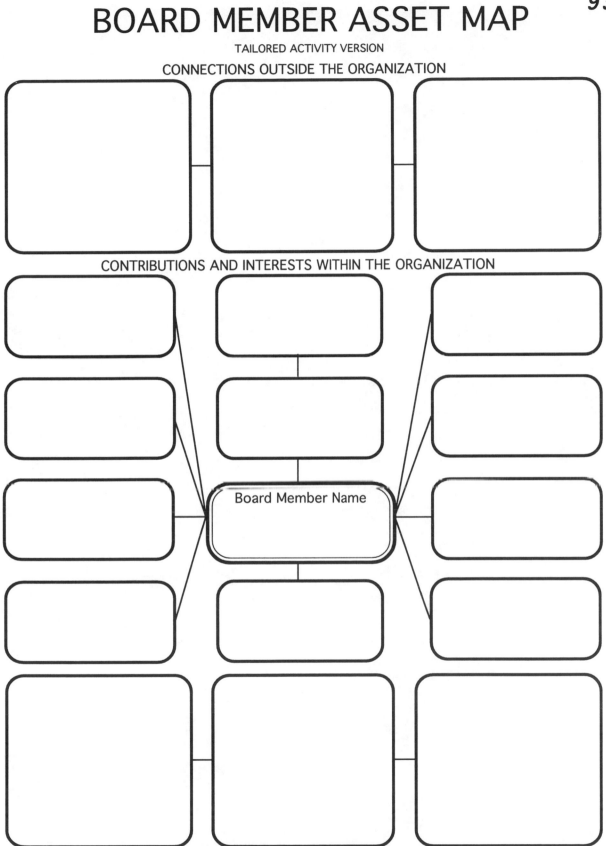

CONTRIBUTIONS AND INTERESTS WITHIN THE ORGANIZATION

Board Member Name

CONNECTIONS OUTSIDE THE ORGANIZATION

BOARD MEMBER ASSET MAP

EXAMPLE

CONNECTIONS OUTSIDE THE ORGANIZATION

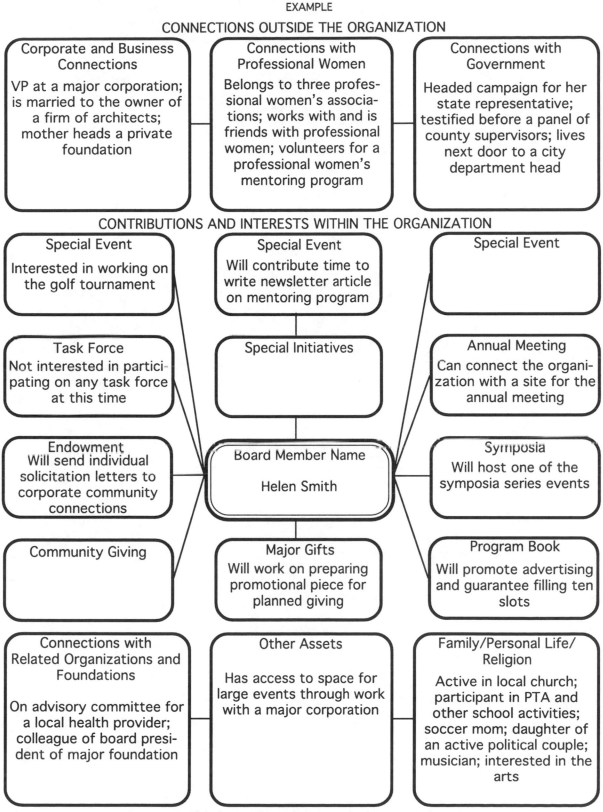

Corporate and Business Connections

VP at a major corporation; is married to the owner of a firm of architects; mother heads a private foundation

Connections with Professional Women

Belongs to three professional women's associations; works with and is friends with professional women; volunteers for a professional women's mentoring program

Connections with Government

Headed campaign for her state representative; testified before a panel of county supervisors; lives next door to a city department head

CONTRIBUTIONS AND INTERESTS WITHIN THE ORGANIZATION

Special Event

Interested in working on the golf tournament

Special Event

Will contribute time to write newsletter article on mentoring program

Special Event

Task Force

Not interested in participating on any task force at this time

Special Initiatives

Annual Meeting

Can connect the organization with a site for the annual meeting

Endowment

Will send individual solicitation letters to corporate community connections

Board Member Name

Helen Smith

Symposia

Will host one of the symposia series events

Community Giving

Major Gifts

Will work on preparing promotional piece for planned giving

Program Book

Will promote advertising and guarantee filling ten slots

Connections with Related Organizations and Foundations

On advisory committee for a local health provider; colleague of board president of major foundation

Other Assets

Has access to space for large events through work with a major corporation

Family/Personal Life/ Religion

Active in local church; participant in PTA and other school activities; soccer mom; daughter of an active political couple; musician; interested in the arts

CONNECTIONS OUTSIDE THE ORGANIZATION

MAPPING VOLUNTEER ASSETS

GOALS ☞

The Goals of this Exercise are:

♦ To think about each volunteer in a multi-dimensional way and develop a more complete view of who the individual really is and what assets he or she represents.

♦ To identify what the volunteer would most like to be doing for the organization and what activities would make the most of his or her assets.

♦ To connect the volunteer's interests and abilities with the most appropriate activities within the organization.

♦ To expand the avenues for contribution to the organization based on what each volunteer brings to the table.

♦ To identify opportunities for volunteer development through training, education, and leadership.

LEARNING
CONCEPTS ☞

The Learning Concepts Associated with this Exercise are:

♦ *Volunteer Assets*—the total of all of the capacities brought to the organization by all volunteers, plus their connections, relationships, and personal potential represent the full measure of volunteer assets.

♦ *Volunteer Capacities*—the specific skills, abilities, interests, and experiences that individual volunteers bring to their work with the organization.

For this exercise, try to think more deeply about who each volunteer really is in terms of the many capacities he or she brings to work with the organization and how each one represents a part of the organization's volunteer assets. Volunteers may be thought of primarily in terms of the specific job they do, and organizations sometimes fail to explore more deeply what contributions each one might make if more were known about them. When an organization succeeds in really knowing its volunteers, it is more able to develop the kinds of opportunities for involvement that will fully utilize and reward each individual. This exercise provides the opportunity to examine volunteer capacities and how they fit into what is happening at the organization, and also to explore how their capacities might be better utilized based on their own interests and potential.

GROUP ACTIVITY

For the group activity, each participant should use a blank copy of the **Volunteer Asset Map (SHOW-21 Version)** included at the end of this section. Group members should spend about 20 minutes thinking independently and filling in the boxes on the worksheet. At the end of this period, all participants should share something about the specific volunteer assets they were able to identify. A discussion can then occur among the group about how much the participants actually know about their volunteers and what they included on their asset map. The discussion should spark new ideas for everyone about what kinds of things may be viewed as volunteer assets.

ORGANIZATIONAL ACTIVITY

The completion of the final volunteer asset map should be accomplished as an internal activity within each organization. This activity may be carried out as an organizational activity, in which case the group may be selected from among whatever parts of the organization seem appropriate, or it may be viewed as an activity most suitable for volunteers to carry out among themselves. The goal is to generate a visual and text-based map of the organization's volunteer assets and capacities. The following questions may be used as a guide for exploring the organization's volunteer assets in an in-depth manner. The written answers to the questions form the text-based asset map; when transferred to the appropriate boxes of the **Volunteer Asset Map (SHOW-21 version)**, a visual version is produced. Once each organization has completed a visual and text version of the map, the working group can come together again to learn about how other participating organizations see their volunteers as assets and how they might mobilize these volunteer assets more fully.

A.   CONTRIBUTIONS AND INTERESTS WITHIN THE ORGANIZATION:

1.   What skills—general and specific—does the volunteer possess? Be sure to explore those skills that may be beyond the scope of the work the volunteer thinks he or she can offer to the organization.

2.   What special qualifications does the volunteer possess? Are volunteers currently using these qualifications in their efforts for the organization?

3.   How much does time does the individual have to volunteer? Would the volunteer prefer to invest more or less time than he or she does currently?

4.   Is the volunteer happiest when working with others or working independently? Is this preference accommodated within the opportunities offered to the volunteer?

5.   What interests—general and specific—does the volunteer possess? Be sure to explore those interests that may be beyond the scope of the work the volunteer thinks he or she can offer the organization.

6.   In which of the organization's programs or activities is the volunteer most interested? Is this preference accommodated within the opportunities offered to the volunteer?

7.   In what ways has the volunteer actually contributed? Might the opportunities offered be changed in order to allow the organization to tap into more of the volunteer's capacities?

B.   CONNECTIONS OUTSIDE THE ORGANIZATION:

1.   What business and corporate connections does the volunteer possess?

2.   What kinds of connections does the volunteer possess with other professionals?

3.   What connections does the volunteer have with government entities?

4.   What connections does the volunteer have with related organizations or other nonprofit foundations?

5.   What assets does the volunteer possess in terms of family connections, activities and relationships in his or her personal life, religious commitments?

6.   What other assets does the volunteer possess in terms of connections outside the organization?

7.   Are these assets in the form of connections outside the organization being utilized to the fullest in terms of the contribution the volunteer makes to the organization?

TAILORED ORGANIZATIONAL ACTIVITY

It is possible that the completion of the final volunteer asset map may be best accomplished by tailoring the process to each specific organization. Each organization is encouraged to make whatever modifications seem appropriate in order to make the most of the asset-mapping process. A completely blank **Volunteer Asset Map (Tailored Activity Version)** suitable for modifying is provided for a more individualized approach to the activity. With this version of the map, each organization can select the categories that best describe its own organizational and community milieus and enter them as headings on the blank map. The guiding questions can then be adjusted to reflect the new headings. Tailored maps also represent a valuable learning tool and can be shared with the larger working group.

APPLICATION

Example 1:

SHOW-21 participants used the Volunteer Asset Map to examine the extent of their knowledge about the individuals who volunteered for their organizations. Most soon realized that they simply did not know enough about their volunteers to be able to use them in the best possible way or to be certain that they were providing the kinds of opportunities that would be most valuable to the volunteers themselves. Most had simply used their volunteers to complete a series of tasks for which the organization required assistance, but little effort had been made to match volunteer assets with organizational opportunities. The participants realized that using some variation of the asset mapping tool could enable them to do a better job of satisfying the people who volunteered for them.

Example 2:

A small nonprofit organization used the Volunteer Asset Map to explore what kinds of things its volunteers might like to do for the organization. It discovered that at least two of its volunteers were interested in working for the organization and were willing to invest volunteer hours to learn the appropriate skills and obtain the necessary qualifications.

VOLUNTEER ASSET MAP

SHOW-21 VERSION

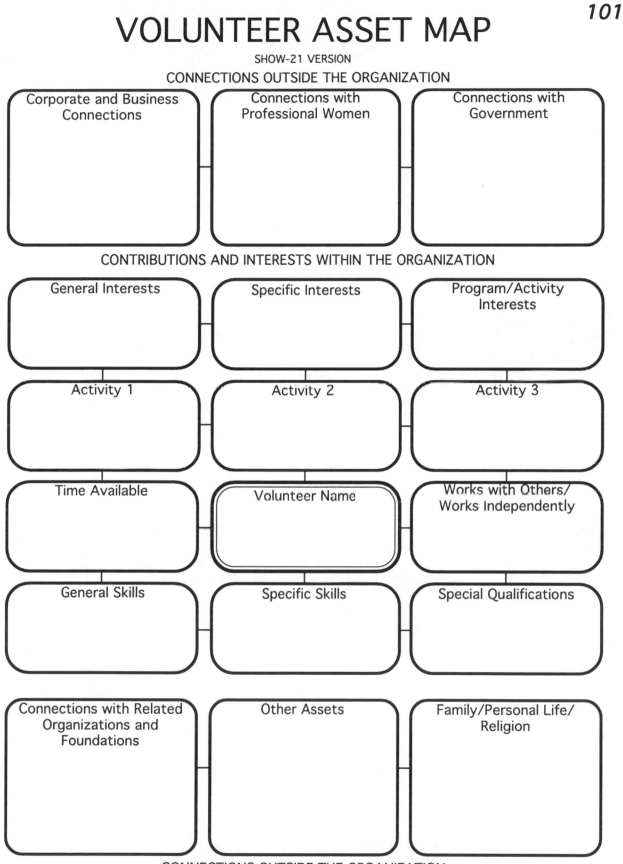

CONNECTIONS OUTSIDE THE ORGANIZATION

Corporate and Business Connections	Connections with Professional Women	Connections with Government

CONTRIBUTIONS AND INTERESTS WITHIN THE ORGANIZATION

General Interests	Specific Interests	Program/Activity Interests

Activity 1	Activity 2	Activity 3

Time Available	Volunteer Name	Works with Others/ Works Independently

General Skills	Specific Skills	Special Qualifications

Connections with Related Organizations and Foundations	Other Assets	Family/Personal Life/ Religion

CONNECTIONS OUTSIDE THE ORGANIZATION

VOLUNTEER ASSET MAP

TAILORED ACTIVITY VERSION

CONNECTIONS OUTSIDE THE ORGANIZATION

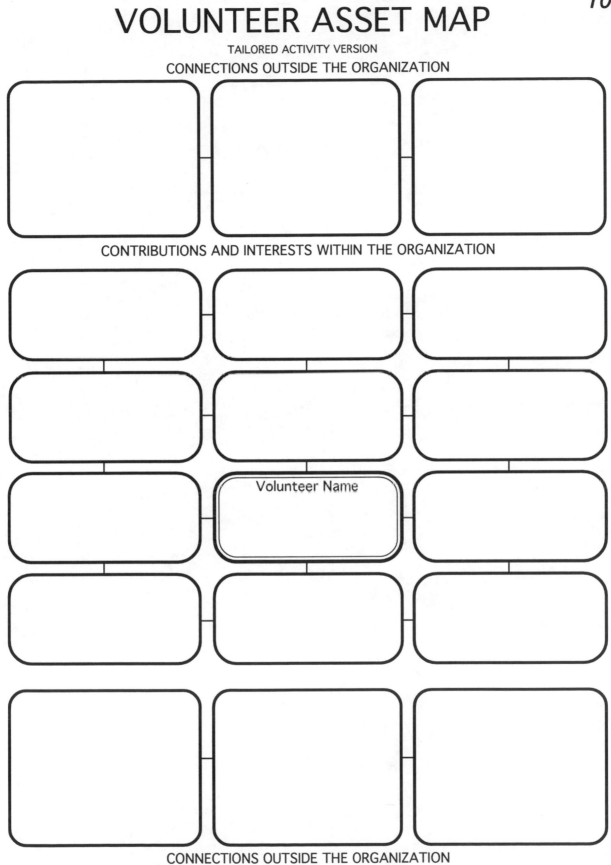

CONTRIBUTIONS AND INTERESTS WITHIN THE ORGANIZATION

Volunteer Name

CONNECTIONS OUTSIDE THE ORGANIZATION

VOLUNTEER ASSET MAP

EXAMPLE

CONNECTIONS OUTSIDE THE ORGANIZATION

Corporate and Business Connections	Connections with Professional Women	Connections with Government
Currently works in the layout and design department of a small publishing house; daughter owns a printing company; neighbor is a manager at large corporation	Member of Chamber of Commerce, design associations, sorority, bridge club, women's club, athletic club, League of Women Voters	Member of the League of Women Voters

CONTRIBUTIONS AND INTERESTS WITHIN THE ORGANIZATION

General Interests	Specific Interests	Program/Activity Interests
Likes people, dislikes repetitive tasks	Has expertise and experience in layout and design work	Wants to be involved in preparing publications and promotional material

Activity 1	Activity 2	Activity 3
Would help with organization's annual report	Would help with annual luncheon brochure	Would help with mailing for capital campaign

Time Available	Volunteer Name	Works with Others/ Works Independently
Works full time; would like to contribute time on specific projects	Betty Martin	Tends to prefer working alone but willing to work on a team

General Skills	Specific Skills	Special Qualifications
Administrative, managerial, design	Layout and design, computer assisted design, publishing and printing	Undergraduate and graduate degrees, 20 years experience

Connections with Related Organizations and Foundations	Other Assets	Family/Personal Life/ Religion
Volunteers for another women's organization; United Way volunteer; member of the board of directors of a small arts organization	Strong connections in the arts	Lives with and cares for elderly mother, collaborates with daughter on design projects, enthusiastic traveler

CONNECTIONS OUTSIDE THE ORGANIZATION

MAPPING CONSTITUENT ASSETS

GOALS ☞

> **The Goals of this Exercise are:**
>
> - To identify all the groups and individuals that comprise the constituency of the organization.
>
> - To think about each individual and group in a multi-dimensional way and develop a more complete view of the constituency and what assets it represents.
>
> - To identify what members of the constituency would most like to be doing for the organization and what activities would make the most of their assets.
>
> - To connect each constituent's interests and abilities with the most appropriate activities within the organization.
>
> - To expand the avenues for contribution to the organization based on what each constituent might bring to the table.
>
> - To identify opportunities for constituent development in terms of training, education, and leadership.

LEARNING
CONCEPTS ☞

> **The Learning Concepts Associated with this Exercise are:**
>
> - *Constituent Assets*—the total of all of the capacities brought to the organization by all constituents, plus the connections, relationships, and personal potential that represent the full measure of constituent assets.
>
> - *Constituent Capacities*—the specific skills, abilities, interests, and experiences that individual and group constituents bring to their work with the organization.

For this exercise, try to think more deeply about who the constituents of the organization really are in terms of the many capacities they bring to their relationship with the organization and how each one represents a part of the organization's constituent assets. Constituents are sometimes thought of primarily in terms of the relationship the organization has with them—as recipients of services, as collaborators on projects, or targets of knowledge and learning—and it sometimes fails to explore more deeply the nature of the relationships that might be developed with them if more about them were known. When an organization succeeds in really knowing its constituents, it is more able to develop opportunities for involvement that will fully utilize and reward each individual or organization that comprises the constituency. This exercise provides the opportunity to examine constituents as assets, and to explore how their capacities might be better utilized based on their own interests and potential.

GROUP ACTIVITY

For the group activity, each participant should use a blank copy of the **Constituent Asset Map (SHOW-21 Version)** included at the end of this section. Group members should spend about 20 minutes thinking independently and filling in the boxes on the worksheet. At the end of this period, participants should share something about the specific constituent assets they were able to identify. A discussion can then occur among the group about the how much participants actually know about their constituents and what they included on their asset map. The discussion should spark new ideas for everyone about what kinds of things may be viewed as constituent assets.

ORGANIZATIONAL ACTIVITY

The completion of the final constituent asset map should be accomplished as an internal activity within each organization. This activity may be carried out as an organizational activity, in which case the group may be selected from among whatever parts of the organization seem appropriate. The goal is to generate a visual and text-based map of the organization's constituent assets and capacities. The following questions may be used as a guide for exploring the organization's constituent assets in an in-depth manner. The written answers to the questions form the text-based asset map; when transferred to the appropriate boxes of the **Constituent Asset Map (SHOW-21 version)**, a visual version is produced. Once each organization has completed a visual and text version of the map, the working group can come together again to learn about how other participating organizations see their constituents as assets and how they might mobilize these assets more fully.

A.   CONTRIBUTIONS AND INTERESTS WITHIN THE ORGANIZATION:

1.   What skills—general and specific—does the constituent possess? Be sure to explore those skills that may be beyond the scope of the involvement the constituent thinks he or she might offer to the organization.

2.   What special qualifications does the constituent possess? Is he or she currently using these qualifications in any efforts on behalf of the organization?

3.   How much does time does the constituent have to participate in organizational activities? Is there a particular amount of time it would be reasonable to ask of the constituent?

4.   Would the constituent be happiest when working with others or working independently? Could this preference be accommodated within the opportunities offered to the constituent?

5.   What interests—general and specific—does the constituent possess? Be sure to explore those interests that may be beyond the scope of involvement the constituent thinks he or she might offer the organization.

6.   In which of the organization's programs or activities is the constituent most interested? Can this preference be accommodated within the opportunities offered to the constituent?

7.   In what ways has the constituent actually contributed already? Might the opportunities offered be changed in order to allow the organization to tap into more of the constituent's capacities?

B.   CONNECTIONS OUTSIDE THE ORGANIZATION:

1.   What business and corporate connections does the constituent possess?

2.   What kinds of connections does the constituent possess with professionals or professional associations?

3.   What connections does the constituent have with government entities?

4.   What connections does the constituent have with related organizations or other nonprofit organizations?

5.   What connections does the constituent have with foundations?

6.   What assets does the constituent possess in terms of family connections, activities and relationships in his or her personal life, religious commitments?

7.   What other assets does the constituent possess in terms of connections outside the organization?

8.   Are these assets in the form of connections outside the organization being utilized to the fullest in terms of the contribution the constituent makes to the organization?

TAILORED ORGANIZATIONAL ACTIVITY

It is possible that completion of the final constituent asset map may be best accomplished by tailoring the process to each specific organization. Each organization is encouraged to make whatever modifications seem appropriate in order to make the most of the asset-mapping process. A completely blank **Constituent Asset Map (Tailored Activity Version)** suitable for modifying is provided for a more individualized approach to the activity. With this version of the map, each organization can select the categories that best describe its own organizational and community milieus and enter them as headings on the blank map. The guiding questions can then be adjusted to reflect the new headings. Tailored maps also represent a valuable learning tool and can be shared with the larger working group.

APPLICATION

Example 1:

A SHOW-21 organization used the Constituent Asset Map to examine how it related to the entire range of its constituency. After completing the asset map, it identified two categories of constituents with which it had only limited relationships. Although the organization had connections in the corporate and business communities, they had not really pursued these relationships or explored how they might be developed to benefit the organization. And while the organization's constituency clearly included government entities, it had not really nurtured its relationships in this domain either. Through completing the asset-mapping process, the organization decided to deliberately target these two areas for building new and stronger relationships.

Example 2:

Another nonprofit organization used the Constituent Asset Map among past recipients of its services to discover whether there was interest on the part of these individuals in remaining involved with the organization following their experience as "client." It found several individuals willing to contribute in an ongoing way by becoming spokespersons for the organization. One was willing to tell the story of her experiences and how the organization helped her for a film clip promoting the organization's work.

CONSTITUENT ASSET MAP

SHOW-21 VERSION

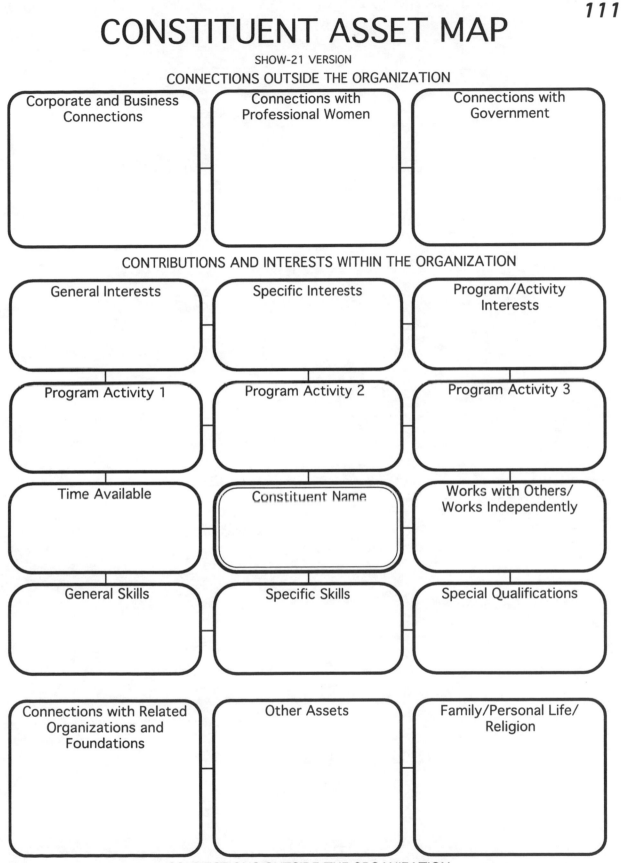

CONNECTIONS OUTSIDE THE ORGANIZATION

| Corporate and Business Connections | Connections with Professional Women | Connections with Government |

CONTRIBUTIONS AND INTERESTS WITHIN THE ORGANIZATION

| General Interests | Specific Interests | Program/Activity Interests |

| Program Activity 1 | Program Activity 2 | Program Activity 3 |

| Time Available | Constituent Name | Works with Others/ Works Independently |

| General Skills | Specific Skills | Special Qualifications |

| Connections with Related Organizations and Foundations | Other Assets | Family/Personal Life/ Religion |

CONNECTIONS OUTSIDE THE ORGANIZATION

CONSTITUENT ASSET MAP

TAILORED ACTIVITY VERSION
CONNECTIONS OUTSIDE THE ORGANIZATION

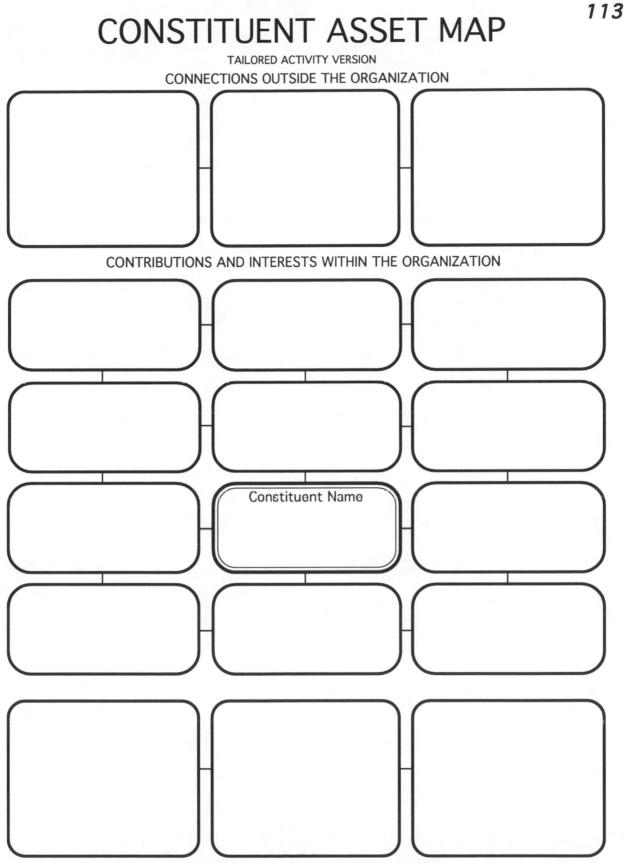

CONTRIBUTIONS AND INTERESTS WITHIN THE ORGANIZATION

Constituent Name

CONNECTIONS OUTSIDE THE ORGANIZATION

CONSTITUENT ASSET MAP

EXAMPLE

CONNECTIONS OUTSIDE THE ORGANIZATION

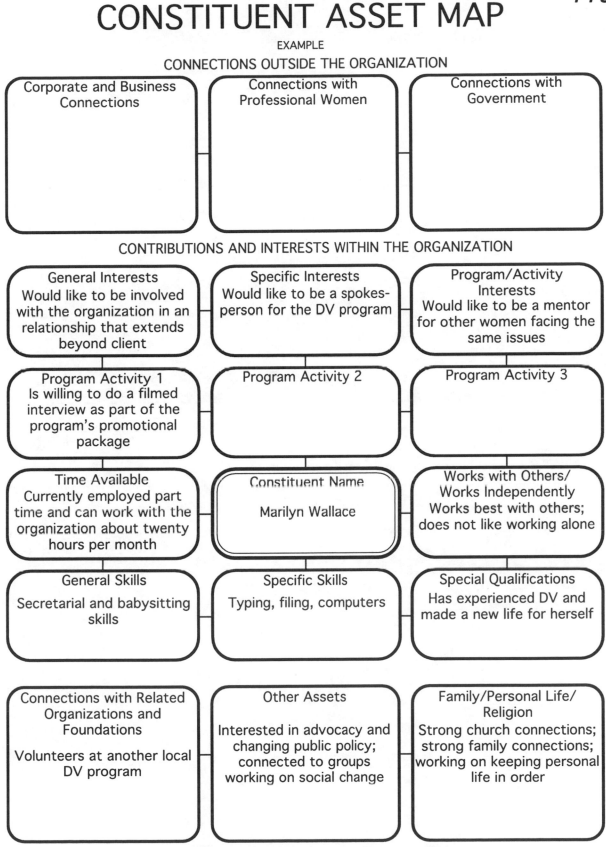

Corporate and Business
Connections

Connections with
Professional Women

Connections with
Government

CONTRIBUTIONS AND INTERESTS WITHIN THE ORGANIZATION

General Interests
Would like to be involved
with the organization in an
relationship that extends
beyond client

Specific Interests
Would like to be a spokes-
person for the DV program

Program/Activity
Interests
Would like to be a mentor
for other women facing the
same issues

Program Activity 1
Is willing to do a filmed
interview as part of the
program's promotional
package

Program Activity 2

Program Activity 3

Time Available
Currently employed part
time and can work with the
organization about twenty
hours per month

Constituent Name

Marilyn Wallace

Works with Others/
Works Independently
Works best with others;
does not like working alone

General Skills

Secretarial and babysitting
skills

Specific Skills

Typing, filing, computers

Special Qualifications

Has experienced DV and
made a new life for herself

Connections with Related
Organizations and
Foundations

Volunteers at another local
DV program

Other Assets

Interested in advocacy and
changing public policy;
connected to groups
working on social change

Family/Personal Life/
Religion
Strong church connections;
strong family connections;
working on keeping personal
life in order

CONNECTIONS OUTSIDE THE ORGANIZATION

MAPPING WHO WE KNOW—SIX DEGREES OF SEPARATION

GOALS ☞

> **The Goals of this Exercise are:**
>
> ◆ To identify all the individuals and groups that comprise the entire connection base of the organization.
>
> ◆ To think about the connection base in an expanded sense, that is, through the idea of "six degrees of separation."
>
> ◆ To think about what advantages might accrue to the organization if efforts were made to tap into the assets from every part of the connection base.

LEARNING
CONCEPTS ☞

> **The Learning Concepts Associated with this Exercise are:**
>
> ◆ *Six Degrees of Separation*—the idea that we are all connected to everyone else on the planet by no more than six degrees of separation. For example, there is one degree of distance between ourselves and the individuals and groups we know personally, two degrees between us and all of the individuals and groups these people know, and so on.

For this exercise, participants should try to think about themselves as connected to every individual and group on the planet, and about the degree to which they are distanced from them. The idea is that six degrees of separation is the maximum, and that everyone can trace themselves to everyone else via a series of no more than six sets of connections. It will not be possible to trace all relationships, but it is a fun exercise to think in these terms and participants will be surprised by the number of important connections they are able to identify. Some of these connections will be potential new relationships for the organization, and thinking about them in a systematic way can open new opportunities for developing them.

GROUP ACTIVITY

For the group activity, each participant should use a blank copy of the **Mapping Who We Know—Six Degrees of Separation (SHOW-21 Version)** tool included at the end of this section. Group members should spend about 20 minutes thinking independently and filling in the boxes on the worksheet. At the end of this period, participants should share something about the connection base they were able to identify within six degrees of separation of themselves. A fun discussion can then occur among group members about just how many and how interesting a set of connections they really have. The discussion should spark new ideas for everyone about the nature of the organization's relationship network and for expanding it.

ORGANIZATIONAL ACTIVITY

The completion of the final map of who people know should be accomplished as an internal activity within each organization. This activity may be carried out as an organizational activity, in which case the group may be selected from among whatever parts of the organization seem appropriate. The goal is to generate a visual and text-based map of the organization's connection base. Serious reflection can then occur about which of the connections it might be reasonable to approach and for what specific purpose. Once each organization has completed its map, the working group can come together again to learn how other participating organizations see their connection base and how they might mobilize these assets more fully.

TAILORED ORGANIZATIONAL ACTIVITY

It is possible that the completion of the final mapping of who we know may be best accomplished by tailoring the process to each specific organization. Each organization is encouraged to make whatever modifications seem appropriate in order to make the most of the asset-mapping process. A completely blank **Mapping Who We Know—Six Degrees of Separation (Tailored Activity Version)** tool suitable for modifying is provided for a more individualized approach to the activity. With this version of the map, each organization can select categories that best describe its own organizational and community milieus and enter them as headings on the blank map. Tailored maps also represent a valuable learning tool and can be shared with the larger working group.

APPLICATION

Example 1:

The Chicago Foundation for Women used the Mapping Who We Know—Six Degrees of Separation tool among its board members to help build enthusiasm for its recent endowment campaign. Board members had fun with the process and were amazed by the number of influential people they were connected to around the globe and by the closeness of most of the connections. Board members were reinvigorated by being able to leave the meeting with new ideas about who they could approach to generate support for the foundation's work.

Example 2:

Another nonprofit organization used the Mapping Who We Know—Six Degrees of Separation tool among staff and board members to identify possible members for a new advisory committee it intended to develop. Because the committee would have specific tasks, the organization wanted to identify a diverse group of individuals who could contribute in particular areas of expertise. Through completing the map of who we know, the organization came up with a long list of individuals it had some degree of connection with as potential committee members.

MAPPING WHO WE KNOW:
SIX DEGREES OF SEPARATION
SHOW-21 VERSION

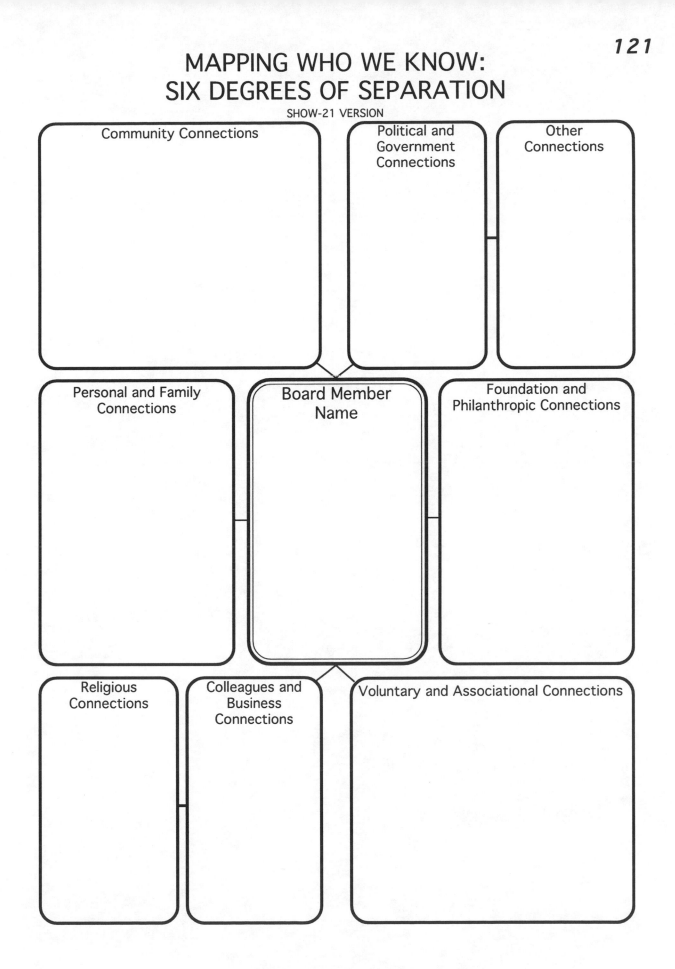

Community Connections

Political and Government Connections

Other Connections

Personal and Family Connections

Board Member Name

Foundation and Philanthropic Connections

Religious Connections

Colleagues and Business Connections

Voluntary and Associational Connections

MAPPING WHO WE KNOW:
SIX DEGREES OF SEPARATION
TAILORED ACTIVITY VERSION

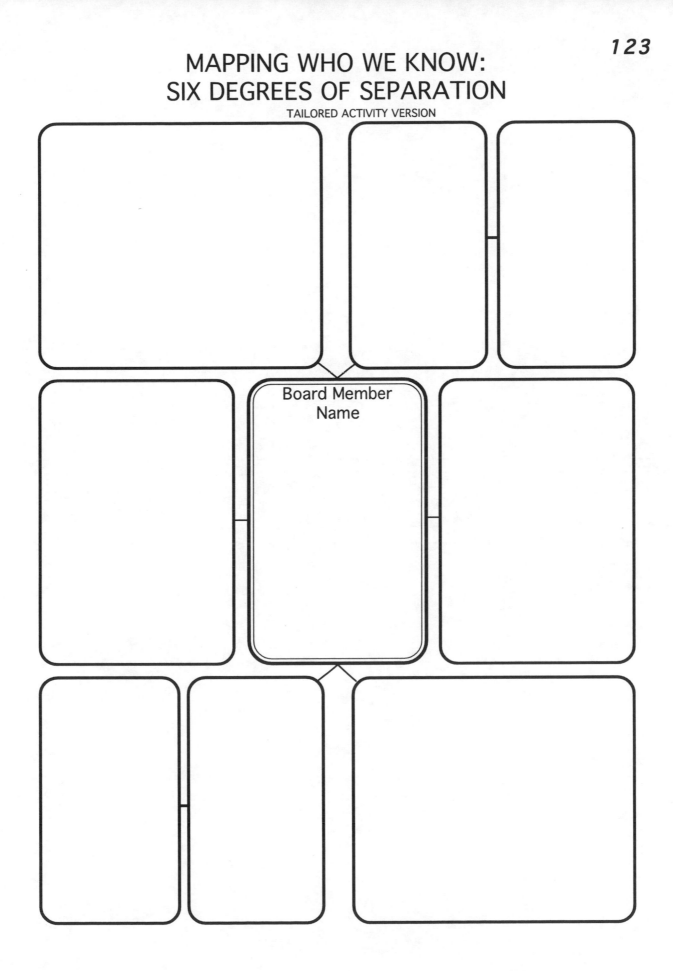

Board Member
Name

MAPPING WHO WE KNOW:
SIX DEGREES OF SEPARATION

EXAMPLE

Community Connections

1 degree: at least 50 people in the community are my personal friends including several state-level bureaucrats, one mayor, three attorneys, one accountant, two physicians; 2 degrees: all of the people my friends know, including a member of Congress

Political and Government Connections
1 degree: Alderman for 10th Ward; 1 degree: members of Governor's Task Force on Welfare Reform; 1 degree: State Representative; 2 degrees: Congressional Representative; 3 degrees: the President

Other Connections

1 degree: people I know from the athletic club where I work out; 2 degrees: at least one movie actor

Personal and Family Connections

1 degree: father well-connected in the corporate world; 1 degree: mother a scholar; 2 degrees: her university and international research connections; 1 degree: uncle a well-known physician; 2 degrees: members of the International Committee on the Status of Child Health; 1 degree: son at Harvard; 2 degrees: the Harvard community of scholars

Board Member Name

Marlena Roberts

Foundation and Philanthropic Connections

1 degree: executive directors of two foundations; 1 degree: Art Institute committee members and director; 2 degrees: director of the local United Way; 3 degrees: directors of national community of United Ways

Religious Connections

1 degree: ministers of six local churches; 1 degree: several hundred church members; 1 degree: head of the National Church of Christ; 2 degrees: international church leaders

Colleagues and Business Connections
1 degree: President and CEO of 2 large corporations; 1 degree: at least 12 business owners in my community; 1 degree: 6 home interior designers; 2 degrees: members of Chamber of Commerce in my community

Voluntary and Associational Connections

1 degree: members of the local interior design association; 2 degrees: national design association membership; 1 degree: local school groups, teachers' organizations, parents' organizations; 1 degree: local outdoor enthusiasts; 2 degrees: Sierra Club membership; 1 degree: staff and constituency of nonprofit where I volunteer; 2 degrees: all the individuals, associations, and institutions they know; 2 degrees: leader of the World Health Organization; 3 degrees: many world leaders

MAPPING OUR STORIES—HOW WE ARTICULATE OUR ORGANIZATIONAL STRENGTHS

GOALS ☞

> **The Goals of this Exercise are:**
>
> ♦ To identify a set of five or six stories about the organization and its mission that exemplify its strengths and contributions.
>
> ♦ To think about how these stories can be articulated in such a way that their meaning is easily conveyed.
>
> ♦ To assure that every person associated with the organization knows these stories and uses them to describe and promote the organization and its work in all kinds of settings.
>
> ♦ Identify ways the organization can incorporate its stories into fundraising efforts.

LEARNING
CONCEPTS ☞

> **The Learning Concepts Associated with this Exercise are:**
>
> ♦ *Organizational Story*—an anecdote about an experience or accomplishment of the organization that effectively illustrates the power of its work.

For this exercise, the group should try to get into a really creative mode and be prepared to talk about their organizations in a series of brief but powerful stories about their accomplishments. Participants should think in terms of having a "library" of five or six such stories that could be used in situations—interpersonal, in print, on film—to describe their organization and its particular strengths.

GROUP ACTIVITY

For the group activity, each participant should use a blank copy of the **Mapping Our Stories—How We Articulate Our Strengths (SHOW-21 Version)** tool included at the end of this section. Group members should spend about 20 minutes thinking independently and filling in at least one of the boxes on the worksheet. At the end of this period, each participant should share one story about his or her organization with the rest of the group.

ORGANIZATIONAL ACTIVITY

The completion of the final map of organizational stories should be accomplished as an internal activity within each organization. This activity may be carried out as an organizational activity, in which case the group may be selected from among whatever parts of the organization seem appropriate. The goal is to generate a map of the organization's stories. Once each organization has developed a set of stories, the working group can come together again to hear them.

APPLICATION

Example 1:

The Chicago Foundation for Women used the Mapping Our Stories—How We Articulate Our Organizational Strengths tool among members of the World Organization of the YWCA. This group was comprised of a large number of women who were trained through the YWCA leadership program and who now hold government and private sector positions in leadership around the world. Through the process of telling their stories, these women realized the extent of the impact the YWCA had on their lives, and recognized how important articulating these stories is for the sustainability of the organization.

Example 2:

Another nonprofit organization used the Mapping Our Stories—How We Articulate Our Organizational Strengths tool among staff members to identify potential "sound bites" for an upcoming media campaign. They identified six stories that each staff and board member learned, and used these stories whenever a newspaper or television reporter interviewed them, and in promotional spots to be aired on the public service stations.

MAPPING OUR STORIES: HOW WE ARTICULATE OUR ORGANIZATIONAL STRENGTHS

SHOW-21 VERSION

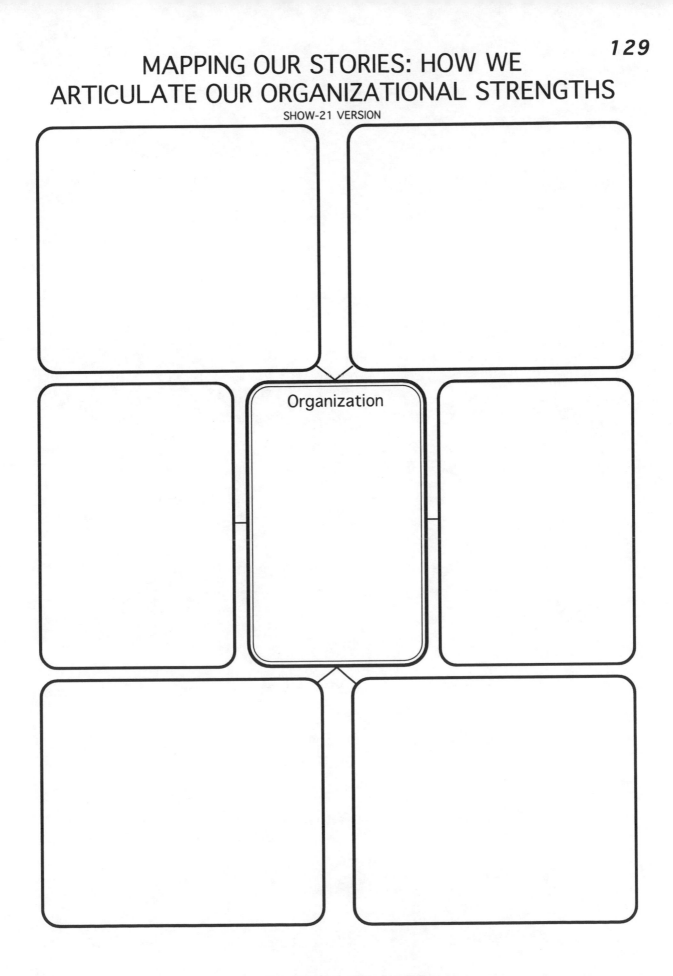

Organization

MAPPING OUR STORIES: HOW WE ARTICULATE OUR ORGANIZATIONAL STRENGTHS

SHOW-21 VERSION

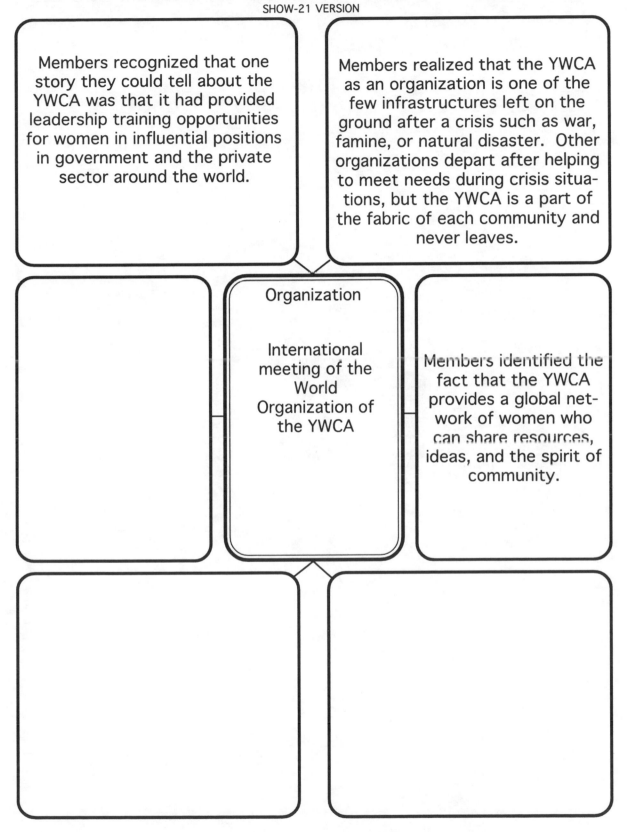

Members recognized that one story they could tell about the YWCA was that it had provided leadership training opportunities for women in influential positions in government and the private sector around the world.

Members realized that the YWCA as an organization is one of the few infrastructures left on the ground after a crisis such as war, famine, or natural disaster. Other organizations depart after helping to meet needs during crisis situations, but the YWCA is a part of the fabric of each community and never leaves.

Organization

International meeting of the World Organization of the YWCA

Members identified the fact that the YWCA provides a global network of women who can share resources, ideas, and the spirit of community.

MAPPING WHAT THE ORGANIZATION HAS TO OFFER TOWARD CREATING BOARD DIVERSITY

GOALS ☞

> **The Goals of this Exercise are:**
>
> ♦ To promote intentionality within the organization about creating a diverse board.
>
> ♦ To identify ways to create a board that is diverse around class, race, ethnic background, gender, sexual orientation, skills, and other characteristics.
>
> ♦ To identify the kinds of opportunities an organization might offer to new board members of diverse backgrounds.
>
> ♦ To recognize that certain kinds of opportunities might not currently be available and to examine whether they could be.

LEARNING CONCEPTS ☞

> **The Learning Concepts Associated with this Exercise are:**
>
> ♦ *Board Diversity*—the mix of board members that appropriately reflects the makeup of the organization's constituents, staff, community, and needs along a variety of personal characteristics. A diverse board reflects the assumption that difference—along many dimensions—is an asset.

For this exercise, try to think more deeply about the kind of diversity the board is hoping to achieve, and what aspects of the organization might be attractive to the new members the board hopes to identify. The members of the SHOW-21 working group generally agreed that it is important to be direct, explicit, and aggressive about locating individuals whose membership will add to the desired board diversity. Relying only on current members to identify friends or acquaintances to fill vacant seats is a method unlikely to build an appropriately diverse board. Open conversation among board members about what groups are unrepresented or underrepresented is an important first step in creating a board with broad representation in terms of race, economic status, and sexual orientation. This exercise provides the opportunity to examine the degree to which the organization's board might be attractive to potential new members.

GROUP ACTIVITY

For the group activity, each participant should use a blank copy of **Mapping What the Organization has to Offer Toward Creating Board Diversity (SHOW-21 Version)** included at the end of this section. Each group member should think about the aspects of his or her organization that might be attractive to new members of the board, in particular in relationship to specific kinds of members they wish to attract. For example, if the goal is to add minority members to the board, the participant should explore what things about the organization might tempt or discourage a potential new member from joining. Will the new board member be the only minority member? Does the organization serve members of the same minority group? What is the culture of the current board and is the new member likely to feel comfortable participating? If the goal is to generate diversity of economic class, the participant should examine such issues as the financial expectations of membership, the location and cost of attending board meetings, and the amount of time a board member is expected to contribute. Group members should spend about 20 minutes thinking independently and filling in as many of the boxes on the worksheet as possible. At the end of this period, each participant should share something about his or her organization that might be attractive to new board members with the rest of the group.

ORGANIZATIONAL ACTIVITY

A more in depth exploration of what the organization has to offer toward creating board diversity should be conducted within each organization by the members of the current board. The goal is to generate a map of what the organization can offer to new board members. Once each organization has completed their map, the working group can come together again to hear what other organizations have identified as potentially attractive to new board members.

APPLICATION

Example 1:

A small nonprofit recognized that its board, although hardworking and committed, did not reflect the demographics of the individuals served by the organization's programs. Hoping to add new minority board members as well as members from the neighborhood in which the organization operated its programs, the board examined what might attract individuals to join them. Board members identified four things that might act as incentives for the new members they hoped to find: (1) the board met at a location in the neighborhood served, thus making board activities accessible to local people; (2) board membership offered access to a variety of influential professionals who worked with them on an advisory without divisiveness or mistrust; and (4) board membership had modest and flexible financial responsibilities attached to it so that lower-income members could afford to participate.

MAPPING WHAT THE ORGANIZATION HAS TO OFFER TOWARD CREATING BOARD DIVERSITY

SHOW-21 VERSION

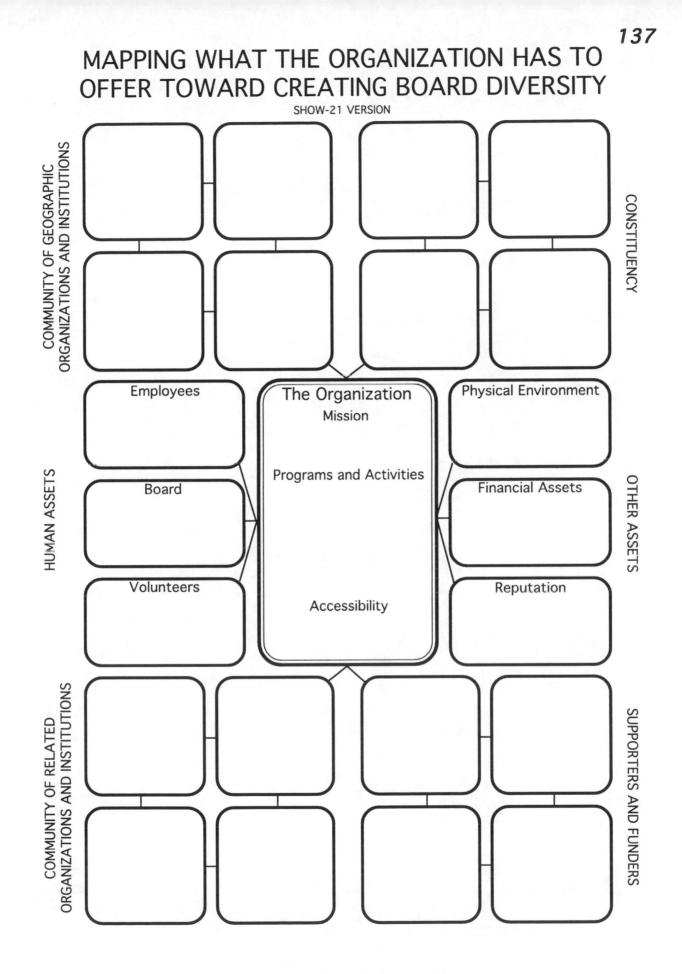

COMMUNITY OF GEOGRAPHIC ORGANIZATIONS AND INSTITUTIONS

CONSTITUENCY

HUMAN ASSETS

OTHER ASSETS

COMMUNITY OF RELATED ORGANIZATIONS AND INSTITUTIONS

SUPPORTERS AND FUNDERS

Employees

Physical Environment

The Organization

Mission

Programs and Activities

Accessibility

Board

Financial Assets

Volunteers

Reputation

© 2000 Chicago Foundation for Women

MAPPING WHAT THE ORGANIZATION HAS TO OFFER TOWARD CREATING BOARD DIVERSITY

TAILORED ACTIVITY VERSION

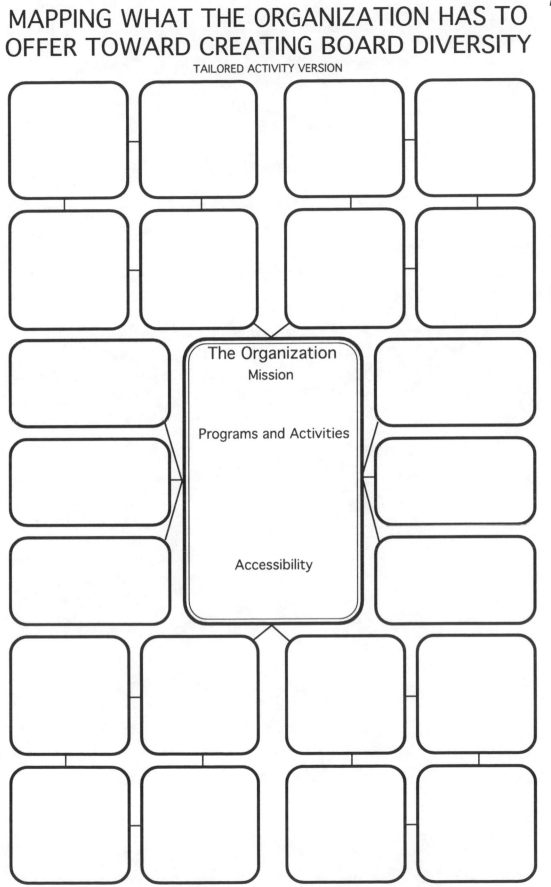

The Organization

Mission

Programs and Activities

Accessibility

MAPPING WHAT THE ORGANIZATION HAS TO OFFER TOWARD CREATING BOARD DIVERSITY

EXAMPLE

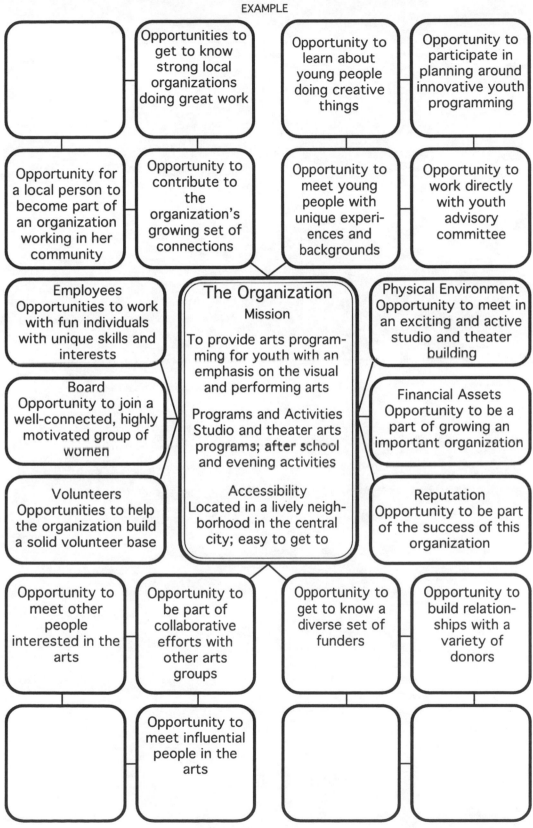

Opportunities to get to know strong local organizations doing great work

Opportunity to learn about young people doing creative things

Opportunity to participate in planning around innovative youth programming

Opportunity for a local person to become part of an organization working in her community

Opportunity to contribute to the organization's growing set of connections

Opportunity to meet young people with unique experiences and backgrounds

Opportunity to work directly with youth advisory committee

Employees
Opportunities to work with fun individuals with unique skills and interests

The Organization

Mission

To provide arts programming for youth with an emphasis on the visual and performing arts

Programs and Activities
Studio and theater arts programs; after school and evening activities

Accessibility
Located in a lively neighborhood in the central city; easy to get to

Physical Environment
Opportunity to meet in an exciting and active studio and theater building

Board
Opportunity to join a well-connected, highly motivated group of women

Financial Assets
Opportunity to be a part of growing an important organization

Volunteers
Opportunities to help the organization build a solid volunteer base

Reputation
Opportunity to be part of the success of this organization

Opportunity to meet other people interested in the arts

Opportunity to be part of collaborative efforts with other arts groups

Opportunity to get to know a diverse set of funders

Opportunity to build relationships with a variety of donors

Opportunity to meet influential people in the arts

SHOW-21 TOOL BOX EVALUATION

SHOW-21 TOOL BOX EVALUATION

The Chicago Foundation for Women would like to thank you for the using this volume and to express the hope that you found its ideas and tools useful in your capacity-building efforts. These final pages offer you the opportunity to evaluate the workbook and tool box, and to return your insights to the foundation so it can incorporate them into this work. The foundation would like to know about both what you thought of the workbook and how you used it. If it is convenient, please return the following questionnaire with your comments to:

The Chicago Foundation for Women
SHOW-21 Workbook Evaluation
230 W. Superior Fourth Floor
Chicago, IL 60610-3536

1.   How would you rate the workbook and its tools overall?

1	2	3	4
Poor	Below Average	Above Average	Excellent

2.   Did you use the workbook in:

1   A group setting?

2   Within your own organization?

3   Both?

3.   Which tools did your organization use? (Circle all that apply)

1   Convening an Organizational Sustainability Working Group
2   Mapping Organizational Assets
3   Exploring Organizational Resiliency
4   Thinking Out of the Box—Mobilizing Organizational Assets
5   Exploring Organizational Sustainability
6   Mapping Employee Assets
7   Mapping Board Member Assets
8   Mapping Volunteer Assets
9   Mapping Constituent Assets
10   Mapping Who We Know—Six Degrees of Separation
11   Mapping Our Stories
12   Mapping What the Organization has to Offer Toward Creating Board Diversity

4.   Which tool did you find to be the most useful and why?

5.   Do you have recommendations for other groups using this workbook and its tools?

6.   What goals does your organization have and how did the tools help you reach these goals?

7.   What stories can you share with other organizations about how these capacity-building tools contributed to your overall sustainability?

THANK YOU FOR TAKING THE TIME TO COMPLETE AND RETURN
THIS EVALUATION